2003

What Is Poetry

Teachers & Writers Books • New York

What Is Poetry

CONVERSATIONS WITH
THE AMERICAN AVANT-GARDE

Daniel Kane

Library of Congress Cataloging-in-Publication Data

Daniel Kane, 1968–
      What is poetry : conversations with the American avant-garde / by Daniel Kane.
            p. cm.
Includes bibliographical references.
      ISBN 0-915924-64-1 (alk. paper)
      1. Poets, American--20th century--Interviews. 2. American poetry--History and criticism--Theory, etc. 3. Experimental poetry, American--History and criticism. 4. Poets, American--21st century--Interviews. 5. Avant-garde (Aesthetics)--United States. 6. Experimental poetry--Authorship. 7. Poetry--Authorship. 8. Poetics
I. Title.
PS325 .K36 2003
810.9'0054--dc21

T&W Books, a division of
Teachers & Writers Collaborative
5 Union Square West, New York, NY 10003-3306

Design: Christina Davis & Christopher Edgar
Cover and text photographs: Ezra Shales

Printed by Thomson-Shore, Inc., Dexter, Michigan.

[acknowledgments]

Author's Acknowledgments: Thanks to Christina Davis and Chris Edgar for their editing and support throughout the production of this book, and to all the poets included here, for their patience, time, and insights during our interviews. Thanks as well to Anselm Berrigan, Mary Giamo McDonnell, and Ezra Shales for their contributions.

Daniel Kane's interviews were conducted over the course of a four-year period, from 1998 to 2002, and originally appeared on the Teachers & Writers website and in *Teachers & Writers* magazine. Readers interested in the entire series of Poets on Poetry interviews (including conversations with Eileen Myles, Lorenzo Thomas, Bill Berkson, and Bob Holman) can access them online at www.twc.org. The interview with Kenneth Koch was originally published in the *Poetry Project Newsletter* #173 (1999).

Teachers & Writers Books wishes to acknowledge the following photographers and publishers for granting permission to reproduce the images that appear in the text: Rae Armantrout, photograph © Nancy Wolfing. John Ashbery, photograph © Sedat Pakay. Robert Creeley, photograph courtesy of New Directions Publishing Corp. and the *Sunday Star*, Auckland, New Zealand. Fanny Howe, photograph © Margaretta Mitchell. Lisa Jarnot, photograph © Tae Wol Stanley. Kenneth Koch, photograph © Larry Rivers, courtesy of Alfred A. Knopf, Publisher. Ann Lauterbach, courtesy of Penguin, photograph © Joyce Ravid. Bernadette Mayer, courtesy of New Directions Publishing Corp., photograph © Marie Warsh. Harryette Mullen, photograph © Judith Natal. Michael Palmer, courtesy of New Directions Publishing Corp., photograph © Norma Cole. Lewis Warsh, photograph © Katt Lissard. Marjorie Welish, photograph © Star Black.

Teachers & Writers Books wishes to acknowledge the following publishers and individuals for granting permission to reprint the poems that appear in the text: John Ashbery, "Honored Guest," from *Your Name Here*. © 2000 by John Ashbery. Reprinted by permission of Farrar, Straus and Giroux, LLC. John Ashbery, "What Is Poetry," from *Houseboat Days*. © 1977 by John Ashbery. Reprinted by permission of Georges Borchardt, Inc., on behalf of the author. Rae Armantrout, "Wake Up," from *Necromance*. © 1991 by Rae Armantrout. Reprinted by permission of the author. Robert Creeley, "Histoire de Florida" (excerpt) from *Life and Death*. © 1998 by Robert Creeley. Reprinted by permission of New Directions Publishing Corp. Fanny Howe, "[Untitled] Creation was the end that preceded means," from *Selected Poems*. © 2002 by Fanny Howe. Reprinted by permission of University of California Press. Lisa Jarnot, "Emperor Wu," from *Some Other Kind of Mission*. © 1996 by Lisa Jarnot. Reprinted by permission of Burning Deck Press. Kenneth Koch, excerpt from "The Pleasures of Peace," from *The Pleasures of Peace*. Reprinted by permission of the Estate of Kenneth Koch. Ann Lauterbach, "(On) Open," from *On a Stair* by Ann Lauterbach. © 1997 by Ann Lauterbach. Used by permission of Penguin, a division of Penguin Putnam Inc. Bernadette Mayer,

Teachers & Writers programs are made possible in part by grants from the National Endowment for the Arts, the New York State Council on the Arts, the New York City Department of Cultural Affairs, the Bronx Borough President and City Council, the Manhattan City Council Delegation, and the Queens Borough President and City Council. Teachers & Writers Collaborative is also grateful for support from the following foundations and corporations: AKC Fund, The Altman Foundation, Axe-Houghton Foundation, The David and Minnie Berk Foundation, The Bydale Foundation, Carnegie Corporation of New York, Catskill Watershed Corp., The Cerimon Fund, Consolidated Edison, E.H.A. Foundation, Fleet Bank, Jenesis Group, Kids II, Inc., Low Wood Fund, Inc., M & O Foundation, NBC, New York Arts Recovery Fund (NYFA), New York Community Trust (Van Lier Fund), New York Times Company Foundation, North Star Fund, The Open Society Institute, Joshua Ringel Memorial Fund, Maurice R. Robinson Fund, Rush Philanthropic Arts Foundation, Salomon Smith Barney (Citicorp Foundation), The Scherman Foundation, Verizon Foundation, The Viburnum Foundation, The Wendling Foundation, and The Willcoxon Family Foundation.

[contents]

For my grandmother,
Sarah Migdal,
and my sister,
Gillian Kane

[introduction]

by Daniel Kane

A few years ago, my grandmother asked me who my favorite poet was. I generally avoid answering such questions, but as it was my grandmother, I figured I'd better answer. Without much hesitation, I replied, "John Ashbery." Naturally, she was eager to know why. "Whenever I read Ashbery, I feel like it's a beautiful day in late spring. I'm on a lush green field—it could be England or Wisconsin—and I'm chasing a rabbit that, strangely enough, isn't moving that fast. Every time I get close to the rabbit, though, it turns around to look at me, wriggles its nose, and darts away from my grasp. Instead of being frustrated by the rabbit's dodging around, I just laugh and continue chasing him. I get lovely exercise, the sun feels great, the weather is temperate, the rabbit adorable, and the laughter gentle and never-ending. But remember, I'm still *chasing,* so there's something difficult going on at the same time that there's something fun happening. And it never ends." After listening to my little rhapsody, my grandmother said, "That sounds really nice. I'd like to read Ashbery."

Poet Ann Lauterbach takes a less pastoral approach to Ashbery's work: she associates reading an Ashbery poem with walking around New York City, where "you might see many people and things and signs and lights that do not belong to each other as much as they do to the city in which you find them."[1] Just as we would never ask a city block full of people to make sense, choosing instead to enjoy the energy and magnificence of the experience, so we must let the luxury of Ashbery's highly complex, intelligent, and often funny free associations carry us along. I think that once we come to accept the fact that there is never a neat ending to an Ashbery poem—that the moment sense is grasped, it immediately and often coquettishly slips away—one can begin to appreciate the joy of reading Ashbery and the poets of the contemporary American avant-garde. In their poems, language is let loose to run around; their work tends to heighten the material nature of the word—its sound, its texture, its potential for multiple and often conflicting meanings, its slipperiness and playfulness—more than it emphasizes language's role in getting solid truths, stories, and lessons across. In a larger sense, these poets could be said to value process: The work isn't there so much to be *understood* as it is to be *experienced.* As Lauterbach so wonderfully put it in our interview, "A poem is not a puzzle to be solved. A poem is an experience, an event, in and of language."

Given the avant-garde's emphasis on free association, wordplay, and process, the interview struck me as the perfect medium to approach the poets featured in this book. The interview is a form that reveals thinking as a process, that shows the mind at work—the poet agrees, disagrees, delays, or refocuses the questions, while the interviewer darts away from a tentative suggestion, makes an outrageous statement, or challenges the author with his own interpretations. The interview, far from ending in definitive conclusion and statement, proves instead to be a kind of partner to the poem, an alternative way of experiencing a complex and satisfying poetics that resists definitive explanation in favor of associative leaps and a deep and ever-present play.[2]

The poets in this book could easily fall under the moniker "postmodern American poets," since they are poets whose work emerged mainly in the 1960s, '70s, and '80s and whose style shares much in common with other postmodern figures including artists, playwrights, filmmakers, and writers like Andy Warhol, Vito Acconci, Kathy Acker, Thomas Pynchon, Richard Foreman, and Elizabeth Murray.[3] I have chosen to call them "American avant-garde poets," however, in order to emphasize their relationship to earlier innovators.

The poetry of the contemporary American avant-garde is heir to an "alternative tradition" that found its genesis in the nineteenth century in the work of Walt Whitman and Emily Dickinson. In the preface to the 1855 edition of *Leaves of Grass*, Whitman wrote, "A great poem is no finish to a man or woman but rather a beginning."[4] This was (and is) a truly radical proposition to make. Consider that most of the popular poetry of Whitman's day was a steady, iambic-pentameter verse filled with great—and often obvious—moral lessons or schoolboy-style adventures. The work of the "Fireside Poets" (William Jennings Bryant, Henry Wadsworth Longfellow, and John Greenleaf Whittier), all of whom were wildly popular in their day, is barely read nowadays. Whitman not only resolutely broke away from the inherited European forms of poetry that the Fireside Poets followed, he also proposed a model for the poem that was defined by its very *openness,* embodied in the idea that a poem is always a "beginning."

Formally speaking, of course, Whitman gave American literature free verse as we know it today. He rejected adhering to a uniform iambic pentameter line, replacing it with a rhythm based partly on the Psalms and Gospels and predicated more on the human breath. Stylistic freedom went hand in hand with freedom of content: Whitman's poetry celebrated homosexuals, prostitutes, and slaves with a candor that had not been seen before, exulting in the body and sexuality with an often explicit and always loving diction. ("How beautiful is candor! All faults may be forgiven of him who has perfect candor"[5]). Such a project set the stage for an alternative American poetry, and the poets who followed Whitman were determined to extend his experiments in form and content. To name just a few surprising examples specific to this book, we should note that Whitman's use of the list (or catalogue) poem[6] has had a profound influence on New York School poets, as we see in Kenneth Koch's poems "One Train" or "Sleeping with Women" and Ashbery's poem "Into the Dusk-Charged Air." Whitman's allusions to rambling and the thrills of the American road have clearly been picked up on by Lisa Jarnot, who in her book *Some Other Kind of Mission* makes all kinds of references to the people, places, and things she sees as she travels across the United States. Whitman's use of parataxis[7] has also been extended in Lewis Warsh's and Harryette Mullen's work. These are just a few of the many examples I could name.

Dickinson's wry humor and telegraphic style, her use of word-play, and her dark, philosophical, and even erotic variations on the hymn likewise proved extremely influential to succeeding innovators.[8] Of the poets in this book, we can see her influence perhaps most clearly in the poetry of Fanny Howe, Harryette Mullen, and Robert Creeley. In her wonderful book *My Emily Dickinson,* poet and critic Susan Howe provides us with a potential reason for Dickinson's ongoing influence on experimental writers:

> By 1860 it was as impossible for Emily Dickinson simply to translate English poetic tradition as it was for Walt Whitman. In prose and in poetry she explored the implications of breaking the law just short of breaking off communication with a reader. Starting from scratch, she exploded habits of standard human intercourse in her letters, as she cut across the customary chronological linearity of poetry.[9]

Starting with Whitman and Dickinson, we can trace a line into the twentieth century: from Whitman's call for a uniquely American literature; to Dickinson's disjunctive style and daring experimentation; to Ezra Pound's slogan "Make it new"; to Gertrude Stein's questioning the very nature of identity through her whimsical statement, "I am I because my little dog knows me"[10]; to William Carlos Williams's "No ideas but in things"; to Charles Olson's exhortation to "get on with it, keep moving, keep in speed...keep it moving as fast as you can, citizen,"[11] we can clearly see the movement away from norms and conventions toward a more fluid poetic model. Note, however, that the poets mentioned here were not upending convention just for the sake of it—we can imagine them agreeing with Pablo Picasso's famous declaration that artists had to know the rules in order to break the rules. For American avant-garde poets, forms and rules were (and are) there to be considered, stretched, and broken; ideas of authorship and sincerity are to be questioned; new ideas, sounds, and dreams that were banging on the door of poetry are finally to be let in.

The Modernist poets—most notably Stein, Pound, and Williams[12]—were in turn read and celebrated by avant-garde writers of the 1950s and '60s. Far from rejecting their recent forebears, the postwar years found poets including Charles Olson and the so-called "Black Mountain" poets[13] (of whom Robert Creeley was a foundational figure), the Beat poets (including Allen Ginsberg, Jack Kerouac, and Gregory Corso), and the New York School poets (including John Ashbery, Kenneth Koch, James Schuyler, Barbara Guest, and Frank O'Hara) talking about, republishing, and reconnecting with their Modernist predecessors.

All of these postwar poets were gathered together in 1960 in Donald Allen's seminal anthology *The New American Poetry*. This book—perhaps more than any other anthology before or since—has proved to have a lasting effect on American poetry, marking a kind of dividing line between those poets who valued innovation first and foremost (the "new" "American" poetry) and poets who still found conventionally linear or narrative approaches worthwhile and pertinent. (We should note that many of the younger writers interviewed in this book credit the Allen anthology for providing them with their initial models and inspiration. Interestingly, Ashbery, Koch, and Creeley, all included in Allen's anthology, have by now proved to be colleagues, teachers, and friends with the younger writers featured here.) At the risk of sounding reductionist, the Allen anthology helped define the line that divides "alternative" and "academic" poetry.

What was "academic poetry"? For the avant-garde, it was the poetry that appeared in the 1957 anthology *New Poets of England and America* (edited by Donald Hall, Robert Pack, and Louis Simpson), which included work by Robert Lowell, W. D. Snodgrass, and Howard Nemerov. *New Poets of England and America* and *The New American Poetry* were pitted against each other in numerous reviews. What's strange about the "academic" vs. "alternative" distinction is that, by 1960, so-called "academic" poets were also using free verse techniques as well as traditional forms and measures. So why the big conflict? For Hall, Pack, and Simpson, "new" tended to mean young poets writing new poems that were narrative-based and on traditional themes. Such poems were interpreted favorably by the dominant literary critics at the time (known as "New Critics").[14] What made the poems in *New Poets* "academic" was the way they employed mythological allusions, a kind of rational take on experience, and a relatively formal "high rhetoric." To put it bluntly, some readers felt that the *New Poets* were writing from a distinctly middle-class, privileged perspective.

Poets in *New Poets of England and America* did not really show the exuberance of Whitman, nor did they build on the radical technique and tone of Dickinson. We would also be hard-pressed to discover any clear affiliation with Pound's, Stein's, Stevens's and Williams's radicalism. On the other hand, *The New American Poetry* presented itself (particularly by the statements on poetics in the back of the book) as a forum for a contemporary avant-garde. In terms of basic content, the poems within broached subjects including drug use, homosexuality, and general chaos. We can look to Allen Ginsberg's fierce depictions of homosexual sex in "Howl," Gregory Corso's wild surrealism, Koch's proclamation "GOOD-BYE, castrati of poetry! farewell stale pale skunky pentameters,"[15] and so forth.

Importantly, the work in *The New American Poetry* was far more experimental formally—in typography, tone, and rhythm—than the poems in *New Poets of England and America*. Of the poems in the Allen anthology, Amiri Baraka said, "The various 'schools' of poetry we related to were themselves all linked together by the ingenuous. They were a point of departure from the academic, from the Eliotic model of rhetoric, formalism, and dull iambics. Bullshit school poetry. All these I responded to and saw as part of a whole anti-academic voice."[16]

While "academic" may not be the appropriate term for the current "literary establishment," the contemporary American avant-garde still has a perceptible anti-establishment bias. For example, you'll note Michael Palmer referring dismissively to the reviewing of poetry in *The New York Times Book Review*, and Kenneth Koch discussing what he calls "the whole 'workshop' kind of poem. 'Grandpa dies on the way to the garage,' or 'I'm having a love affair with a student,' or something." The line dividing academic (or mainstream) poetry from avant-garde poetry, while increasingly blurry, certainly still exists.

My admittedly fast and loose trot through the history of the American avant-garde in poetry is hardly complete. Rather, I am simply emphasizing the "American" aspects of the avant-garde. If I were to open the floodgates, the influences would also certainly include French poets Charles Baudelaire, Guillaume Apollinaire, and Max Jacob—their experiments with visual and verbal forms of poetry, urban content, and blurring of boundaries between poetry and prose clearly exerted a strong influence on the American avant-garde poets that I interviewed. Indeed, New York School poet Ron Padgett argues that an avant-garde tradition can be traced back from

> O'Hara, Koch, Ashbery, Schuyler, Elmslie, Ginsberg, Cesaire, to Kenneth Patchen, Hart Crane, Williams, Pound, Stevens, to early Eliot, Lorca, Mayakovsky, Neruda, the Surrealists, the Dadaists, Hopkins, Apollinaire, Jacob, Reverdy, Cendrars, Larbaud, St-Pol-Roux, Mallarme, Lautréamont, Rimbaud, Baudelaire, Whitman, Dickinson, Hölderlin, Blake, Ariosto... let's go back to Aristophanes![17]

So far, I've been referring to the poets in the American avant-garde as if they could all naturally (if loosely) be grouped together. I would like to devote the rest of my introduction to considering the techniques, strategies, and concerns that the contemporary American avant-garde poets have in common, including the blending of "high" and "low" language, the blurring of the lines between prose and poetry, the enthusiastic use of humor, the employment of collage techniques, the transformation of traditional forms, and political content.

High Meets Low: Rhetorical Strategies

Practically all the poets in this book navigate between "high" and "low" discourses in their work, mixing high rhetoric with the colloquial. The incorporation of apparently "everyday" words and phrases is a deliberate choice, one that helps these poets blend realities in a fun, useful, even political way. Note, for example, John Ashbery's delight in using recondite words and phrases (*hod-carrier, lacustrine, postillion*) alongside down-to-earth language (*macaroni, nerd,* "dem days is gone forever"). Marjorie Welish leavens an often dense, theoretically-determined diction with phrases like "across a wall is a something." Ann Lauterbach employs such archaic phrases as "the goodly weeds" beside pop phrases like "girl meets boy." In Bernadette Mayer's book *Midwinter Day* and in Lewis Warsh's book *Part of My History,* at times awe-inspiring language appears side by side with the flat reportage of what they had for breakfast and who they chatted with on the phone.

This mixture of high and low rhetoric has a rich tradition behind it. In Lord Byron's mock-epic *Don Juan,* for instance, lighthearted commentary is expressed within an ottava rima stanza. Byron was, of course, playing on the fact that the ottava rima is associated with the lofty epic tradition, dating back to Boccaccio:

> In Seville was he born, a pleasant city,
> Famous for oranges and women—he
> Who has not seen it will be much to pity,
> So says the proverb—and I quite agree;
> Of all the Spanish towns is none more pretty,
> Cadiz perhaps—but that you soon may see;
> Don Juan's parents lived beside the river,
> A noble stream, and call'd the Guadalquivir.[18]

Such a funny use of ottava rima finds an interesting update in Kenneth Koch's *Ko, or a Season on Earth* (a mock-epic about a Japanese baseball player), which also pokes fun at high rhetoric.

In the early twentieth century, we find this juxtaposition of high and low evolving in many ways. T. S. Eliot's *The Waste Land,* for instance, places classical diction ("Those are pearls that were his eyes") side by side with conversational vernacular ("He'll want to know what you done with that money") and quasi-ragtime lyrics ("O O O O that Shakespeherian

Rag—"). In "This Is Just to Say," William Carlos Williams takes this medley of high and low to a different level: that of the form itself. He tests our "high" idea of a poem by placing it in the form of a note left on a refrigerator. The poets of the Harlem Renaissance also consciously mixed high and low diction. In Langston Hughes's poem "The Weary Blues," for example, we find the blues lament of an old Negro reframed within the context of a relatively formal, rhyming poem:

> In a deep song voice with a melancholy tone
> I heard that Negro sing, that old piano moan—
>   "Ain't got nobody in all this world,
>   Ain't got nobody but ma self.
>   I's gwine to quit ma frownin'
>   And put ma troubles on the shelf."[19]

I've always read this poem as a petition to the reader arguing that colloquial diction can carry just as much emotional and intellectual power as "high" diction. In any case, there's a wonderful tension here between what constitutes our understanding of both the "popular" and the "literary." My point here is to emphasize how the poets in this book are working within a tradition that has functioned to destabilize the boundaries that keep "high" culture safe from "low" culture. American avant-garde poets—like Byron, Williams, and Hughes before them—all work against maintaining a sense of elite culture in distinction to mass culture.

Border Crossing: Prose Poetry

The poets in this book challenge yet another distinction: the borderline between poetry and prose. Blurring the margins between these two genres, not surprisingly, challenges our notions of what poetry is.

Fanny Howe, for instance, says that she considers the poem to be a single sentence, and that the sentence itself is characterized by musical attributes that she calls "sound-lines." Michael Palmer and John Ashbery often include prose sections in books that also contain more conventional lyrics. Ann Lauterbach's, Marjorie Welish's, and Robert Creeley's experiments with syntax, grammar, and line breaks often lead us to question the distinctions between written and spoken speech, and the poetic stanza and prose paragraph. Such a range of tones works to resist the reader's organizing impulse to recognize and impose a familiar unitary "voice" onto a writer's text. It is also a way in which these poets continually challenge themselves as writers: listen to Kenneth Koch encourage his students to "write short plays, prose poems, transform an article in a newspaper into a poem . . . write sestinas . . . break away from 'poetry' poetry." Because innovation and a widening of possibilities is a kind of shared standard among this group of writers, letting prose horn in on poetry is a fruitful way to play around and to ask very real and serious questions at the same time.

Again, tradition is not invisible here. There is a great history to the prose poem, one that emphasizes the fun and radical nature of the rule-breakers. We could point to earlier French practitioners of the prose poem such as Charles Baudelaire, Arthur Rimbaud, and Max Jacob. We might also point out Gertrude Stein's work, especially the series of prose poems collected in her book *Tender Buttons* (an undeniable influence on the work of many of the writers in this book). Stein was especially able to imbue the prose stanza with a fantastic sense of rhythm and magnificent aural effects—ingredients we'd ordinarily associate with the lyric.

Of the poets in this book, Rae Armantrout may be one of the most committed to experimenting with prose values in poetry. I like to think of Armantrout's prose poems and prose-like lines as her way of defying convention. I think this stems partly from her upbringing: Armantrout was brought up in a fundamentalist Christian household, and came to reject the strict orthodoxy for a more flexible and questioning approach to experience. Indeed, we can detect in her poetry a consistently rebellious response to events that are ordinarily accepted as given. In her poem "Anti Short-Story," for example, we have the following deceptively simple lines:

> A girl is running. *Don't* tell me
> "She's running for a bus."
>
> All that aside![20]

This text captures Armantrout's refreshing refusal to do what she's told. A girl might be running, but because this act is veering into cliché (as suggested by the line "She's running for a bus"), Armantrout assumes a sort of comic attack mode, displacing the cliché by her imperative "*Don't* tell me." We end up not knowing why or where the girl is running. Additionally, the prosaic lines in this poem counter our intuitive expectation for a more lyrical tone—they also contradict the "anti" in "anti short-story" by sounding suspiciously like the beginning of a short story! Here we see how prose values can, in a fun and complex way, alter our notions about how a poem should look and sound, making us as readers come up with our own answers.

Tongue in Cheek: Humor, Parody, and Wordplay

You've probably noticed how often the words *play* and *fun* keep cropping up. This is because humor is so significant for the avant-garde, serving both as an antidote to high seriousness as well as a method in itself. Humor is often a challenge to convention, propriety, and established hierarchy— just think of hearing a loud belch during an opera, or witnessing one's high school teacher sitting on a whoopee cushion.

The poets in this book use humor to achieve these aims and others. Lewis Warsh, who writes about such gloomy subjects as the ongoing alienation between people, uses a deeply ironic humor to serve as a kind of detached counterpoint to the often pained observations in his poems. While Warsh's lines may make us feel melancholy ("I think it's important to experience the act of adultery at least once / There's always someone waiting in the wings to take your place"[21]), they do not slip into downright bathos, maintaining a liveliness and tension that keep us from taking the implicit narrator in these lines too seriously.

Humor also has a strong connection to wordplay. Read through Harryette Mullen's poems in *Sleeping with the Dictionary*, which is literally packed with jokes, puns, and wisecracks. As a child, Mullen's favorite poems were of the humorous, tongue-twisting variety: Edward Lear's hilarious, surreal poetry ("There was an Old Man with a beard, / Who said, 'It is just as I feared! / Two Owls and a Hen, / Four Larks and a Wren, / Have all built their nests in my beard!'"[22]) or Lewis Carroll's richly textured lines ("'Twas brillig, and the slithy toves / Did gyre and gimble in the wabe"[23]). The ensuing laughter in the face of such nonsense words and neologisms helps us see that language is always on the verge of falling apart. Language, as Lear, Carroll, and Mullen make clear, is elastic enough to give us unexpected delights and pleasures free from the authority of logic and common sense.

Perhaps the most seriously laugh-out-loud poet in this book is Kenneth Koch, but again, humor, for Koch, is hardly an end in itself. In our interview, Koch emphasized how he read Max Jacob and "learned how to be comic and lyrical at the same time. That was quite a discovery. It helped the determination to get rid of Eliot, and depression, and despair, and inky-dinky meter." In other words, humor is a *method* to divest oneself from poetic convention and break free toward a fresher conception of poetic language.

One specific method Koch employed to inject a high comic mode into contemporary poetry was to write apostrophic poems. (His book *New Addresses* is composed entirely of apostrophic poems—poems addressed to "kidding around," to his father's business, to Jewishness, and other surprising subjects.) According to the *Princeton Encyclopedia of Poetry & Poetics*, apostrophe leads the poet "away from the generality of listeners or readers to address a specific reader, a character in the narrative, or some other person, thing, or idea."[24] Koch takes the apostrophic turn to the extreme, conversing with a staggering variety of inanimate objects, vague feelings and gestures, and philosophical thoughts. Koch's apostrophic addresses can also be playful and wildly funny, all the while making them personal and emotionally charged (these from both early and recent books):

> Bananas! piers, limericks! [...] Sea, sea you! ("Sun Out")
> O closet of devoted airplanes ("When the Sun Tries to Go On")
> O red-hot cupboards and burning pavements ("En l'an trentiesme de mon âge")
> Blue air, fresh air, come in, I welcome you, you are an art student ("Fresh Air")
> O launch, lunch, you dazzling hoary tunnel / To paradise! ("Lunch")
> Yet sometimes you are breathtaking, / Kidding around! ("To Kidding Around")

Here Koch is expanding the possibilities of what can be addressed in a poem. As in previous instances, we should note that he is also extending an established poetic tradition. Think of nineteenth-century apostrophic poems such as William Blake's "The Sick Rose" or Percy Bysshe Shelley's "Ode to the West Wind," or twentieth-century apostrophes including Edna St. Vincent Millay's "Spring" ("To what purpose, April, do you return again? / Beauty is not enough"[25]), Hart Crane's "To Brooklyn Bridge" ("And Thee, across the harbor, silver-paced"[26]), Marianne Moore's "To a Steamroller," and Frank O'Hara's "A True Account of Talking to the Sun at Fire Island." We might conclude that Koch somehow absorbed these historical forms and—with the wacky energy that they instilled in his imagination—was encouraged to create some of the most inventive and funny apostrophes in twentieth-century poetry.

Mixing It Up: Collage, Fragments, and Juxtaposition

A further common method—one that goes hand in hand with mixing up dictions, making things funny, and blurring the lines between prose and poetry—is collage. The term—and literary method—is, of course, adopted from the visual arts. There is a great early-twentieth-century tradition of collage in art, including the mixed-media assemblages of Marcel Duchamp, Pablo Picasso's cubist paintings, and the work of Max Ernst. These artists in turn influenced their own contemporary avant-garde writers: Gertrude Stein, Guillaume Apollinaire, and André Bréton, to name just three.

In poetry, collage most often means using found material, lines and phrases literally lifted from other people's work and grafted into one's own. The specific use and meaning of found material varies. Note, for example, Ashbery: "I frequently incorporate overheard speech, which there's a lot of in New York City"[27]; Lewis Warsh: "Collage plays a big role—disparate units side by side"; Robert Creeley "[Collage is] like quoting in jazz and lets one set an echo, tonal, rhythmic or otherwise, quickly into the pattern."

The brash act of taking other people's property and calling it your own has a political aspect as well: it's both subversive and democratic. Collage prompts us to think about the very nature of language and identity. It also reveals new things to the author. For example, Lisa Jarnot explains in our interview that most of the poetry in *Some Other Kind of Mission* "comes from the *I Ching*. A lot of it comes from a recording I have between Bob Dylan and an obsessed fan of his. There's also the refrain 'like they say,' which is a phrase Robert Creeley sometimes uses in his poems." Regarding the results, Jarnot added, "Collage helped me see how certain material might be related to my life or my personal narrative at a given point." Here Jarnot acknowledges the constructed (collaged, cobbled together) nature of her self, her narrative. Collage is both the exterior experience one has of the world and an interior choice one makes to determine and shape one's relationship to that world.

Collage, moreover, offers the poet a bigger toolbox to work with: the whole world independent of our own supposedly "original" thoughts and expressions becomes potential source material. This is a very twentieth-century phenomenon, in which poetry parallels other art forms—cutting, quoting from, and synthesizing various previously distinct and independent styles, sounds, and voices is characteristic of what we might call postmodernism. Think about all the other so-called postmodern arts that have benefited from integrating popular culture and other art forms: Robert Rauschenberg's various sculptures that are composed of chicken wire and found scraps of paper and wood, or Andy Warhol's lifting images of car crashes from newspapers. Think of modern jazz, where you can hear a soloist incorporating melodies from a variety of sources into his or her solo (say, John Coltrane's use of the melody "My Favorite Things"), or what DJs do on practically any hip-hop album, where bits of other songs are collaged into the overall mix. In all these cases, collage offers us the provocative joys of juxtaposition and mysteriousness while encouraging us to think about what constitutes authority, identity, voice, originality, sincerity, and art. There is no good reason poetry should not be in on the fun, as Lisa Jarnot and so many other poets in this book recognize.

Breaking the Rules: Formal Experimentation

What are the attitudes of the avant-garde writer—always wanting to "make it new"—to the sonnet, the sestina, the canzone? As contradictory as it might sound, most of the poets in this book have shown a real commitment to writing in traditional forms and meters.

Kenneth Koch, for example, experimented with all kinds of forms. In addition to *Ko, or a Season on Earth*, he also used ottava rima in *The Duplications*.[28] John Ashbery has likewise experimented a great deal with formal poetry—he's written sestinas, including the famous "Farm Implements and Rutabagas in a Landscape" and "The Painter," as well as canzones and pantoums. Ashbery even slipped in a double sestina into his book-length free verse opus, *Flow Chart*. A double sestina would traditionally stand alone (like Swinburne's double sestina "The Complaint of Lisa," whose end-words Ashbery swiped for his own double sestina!), so people can point to it and exclaim about its technical brilliance and so on. The fact that Ashbery sneaks a double sestina into a vast, free verse extravaganza of a book is, in a way, poking fun at the seriousness of the form—while abiding by its rules. It's almost as if the poetic forms are parodies of order—sort of like marching around in uniform while singing Judy Garland songs. The younger poets in this book continue extending the boundaries of the formal poem. Lisa Jarnot writes sestinas, for example, and

Harryette Mullen writes what she calls "kinky quatrains" in her book *Muse & Drudge,* lightened with double entendres, puns, and polysemic wordplay.

Bernadette Mayer's relationship with the sonnet is particularly interesting. People have laughed, shouted at, and argued with each other about whether Mayer is really writing sonnets—probably because the sonnet is the most widely read (and revered) poetic form. The sonnet's formal rules not only determine its shape and action but also demarcate what kinds of expression are appropriate to it. In the Petrarchan sonnet, for example, stanzas are divided into an octave and a sestet with an attendant rhyme scheme of *abbaabba* and *cdecde* or *cdcdcd*. The two stanzas represent a two-part division of thought as it pertains to a beloved, where the octave "offers an admirably unified pattern and leads to the *volta* or 'turn' of thought in the more varied sestet."[29] In a nutshell, the form brings up a question or theme in the first part, and then comes to a satisfying conclusion in the second. Yet the sonnet has hardly been a stable form historically. It has always been open to change, even when it comes to the rigid rhyme scheme. While the sonnet began in Italy, the sixteenth-century sonnet as it was written in England introduced new rhyme schemes including *abab cdcd efef gg*. And, since English contains fewer similar-ending words than Romance languages, William Shakespeare, John Donne, Mary Wroth, and others tended to introduce a more varied music into the sonnet, placing less emphasis on rhyme.

Twentieth-century poets continued to introduce progressive changes to the form—one can find strictly rhymed, blank verse, unrhymed, internally rhymed, and every-now-and-then rhymed sonnets. Especially interesting are the experimental sonnets penned by e. e. cummings, Kenneth Patchen, Edwin Denby, and Ted Berrigan. For some additional twists, one might also want to take a look at sonnets by Edna St. Vincent Millay, Rainer Maria Rilke, and Gwendolyn Brooks.

Even though Mayer claimed the sonnet allows one to "come to a conclusion," she also pointed out the artificiality of such a goal by adding, "Sonnets *pretend* to reflect the way you think. That's always been my theory." She (like other avant-garde poets) seems obsessed with the questions: How do we think? Can we trust the words we use to "naturally" and transparently represent what we're thinking? Mayer and others like to undress traditional notions of closure, and firmly believe that the poet is much better off not knowing where the poem will end.

When I asked Mayer, "What if William Shakespeare were to walk up to you one day and ask you, 'Bernadette, how does your poem fit into the definition of the word *sonnet?*'" she responded, "I'd say, 'William, it has fourteen lines!' And then he'd probably say, in a dubious kind of tone, 'Yeah, fourteen lines.'" As events in life tend not to have neat endings, so Mayer turns the sonnet into a form that may evoke order, but also refuses it.

The Art of the Politic: Radical Aesthetics

It is probably readily apparent by now that in the "tradition" of the avant-garde, formal innovations often go hand in hand with progressive political ideas, and that it's no accident I've used words like "free" and "radical" so much. As Michael Palmer says in our interview: "The vast majority of poets of roughly my generation identified strongly with the Civil Rights movement, the anti-war movement during the Vietnam period, as well as feminism, gay liberation, and anti-colonialism. . . . There was certainly a many-faceted, eclectic attempt to justify a radical aesthetics in terms of these issues and positions." In the work of avant-garde poets, these "radical aesthetics" are manifest in an often fragmented and resolutely non-narrative verbal style, a sense of an unstable or fluid identity, and a blurring of the lines between poetry and prose. Such an aesthetics aims the reader toward a conception of language that is free from linearity and fixed notions of what constitutes truth, order, and meaning.

One poet in this book who has explored the links between political radicalism and formal innovation for much of her career is Fanny Howe. She even rejects titles to encourage "Freedom at any cost!" and the subject-position of the author is qualified by a more impersonal subject that serves to question the very meaning of what an "individual" is. As Howe writes in *Artobiography,* she strives "to abolish the personal, or hurl it to the furthest point; and polish the impersonal, until its dazzle unfocuses complete clarity, as with everything good."[30] Unlike more traditional political poetry, you'll find that Howe's poetry does not condense and explain—rather, it *unfocuses* in order to capture, if only for a fleeting moment, the political nature of a constantly changing world. It invites us through its spiritual, intellectual, political, and often funny impulses to initiate an ongoing conversation.

Harryette Mullen's use of dislocative techniques is also inherently political, especially as regards fixed notions of identity. Mullen complicates assumptions of what it means to have a "black voice" through strategies including wordplay, punning, parataxis, cryptographic writing, and anagrams. These formal experiments work to challenge conventional definitions of voice and subject—whether that subject is "gendered" as man or woman, or "raced," etc. The first few lines of Mullen's prose poem "Elliptical" offer a good example of this:

> They just can't seem to… They should try harder to … They
> ought to be more … We all wish they weren't so … They
> never… They always … Sometimes they …Once in a while
> they … However it is obvious that they … Their overall ten-
> dency has been … The consequences of which have been …
> They don't appear to understand that …[31]

This is a poem that relies on what is not said to get some real meanings across. As I read it, the ellipses here represent the unspoken, tentatively uttered prejudices of well-meaning white folk who, you know, wish African-American people well but just can't understand why they are all …you know.…. Mullen's text is pleasurably complex in that the reader is invited to participate in the poem—through the "game" of filling in the blanks—in a way that does not occur in message-bearing poems. To keep the silences present through ellipses (what the speaker is *really* thinking) is to gently force us as readers to fill in the blanks, and subsequently to question our own complicity in a not-so-benign racism that universalizes black people into an undifferentiated *they*.

Before moving on, I would like to emphasize that one might fruitfully explore the work of *all* the poets in this book by considering the political implications of their poetics. Refer, for example, to Lisa Jarnot's suggestion in our interview: "I think I would say that one doesn't have to depend on—or be surrounded by—high culture to be a poet." Consider Marjorie Welish's question: "What are the creative implications for possible worlds in which only definitions exist or only descriptions exist?" Think about Robert Creeley's statement: "Whatever one may have meant the construction to mean or say, the experience of others will also be a large factor in the stabilization of such 'meaning.' Wars have many 'meanings' for those involved with them—as do poems, as do people. 'Everybody's right,' as Ginsberg said." The poems these writers produce are intended, in part, to serve as alternative models for a progressive and flexible poetics/politics.

"I" Is An Other: The Destabilized "I"

In our interview, Lewis Warsh makes the statement, "Identity is often slippery, and the way I write is only synonymous with who I am at the moment." Warsh is not alone in his concept of identity. One of the most profound links between these avant-garde writers is the fact that all of them eschew concepts of "natural" voice in favor of a more fluid and complex vision of what constitutes authorship, power, and the individual. Read the following excerpts from the interviews and note what they say about these poets' relationship to the "authorial I":

> **Palmer:** I'm not sure I've ever actually met the author. The author passes through my life, a kind of presence-absence, but we do not speak. Maybe I get an occasional glimpse in dreams [...] but he/she never joins me for morning coffee. When I go to the market or roam the streets, I will sometimes imagine a tap on the shoulder, or hear a whisper, but when I turn around no one is there.

> **Mullen:** For me, race, class, and gender have been significant issues, but of course they are not the whole of identity, and certainly they are not the sum of my poetry, or of anyone's poetry for that matter. I can be a black woman while chewing gum and thinking about Disneyland or supermarkets, while reading Stein or Shakespeare, just as I can be a black woman contemplating conventional representations of black women in literature, media, and popular culture.... Whatever the content of the poem, identity (not just my own) is as much an aspect of the work as a concern with language, poetics, and form.

> **Ashbery:** But one doesn't know anything! That's the problem.

In sum, these comments reflect the notion that the place of the Romantic poet as mediator of truth and experience is simply no longer tenable to the contemporary American avant-garde. If "one doesn't know anything," then we are left to construct a semblance of the real with the objects and stimuli that we have arbitrarily in front of us. Even racial identity—as is apparent in Mullen's work—is composed, structured, *made up.* This does not mean that identity is therefore unreal. Rather, it means that we must treat identity in a far more flexible way than one might otherwise think possible. As Mullen insists in our interview, "I don't know if I'm undermining identity so much as continually rewriting and revising it."

It is interesting to consider this stance's connection not only to collage, but also to abstraction in the visual arts. Many of the writers collected here (especially Ashbery, Koch, Jarnot, Creeley, Mayer, Lauterbach, and Welish) were or continue to be involved with the visual arts. One aim of abstract painting, particularly "action painting," was (and is) to engage and release the unconscious of the artist. In a letter to Charles Olson, Robert Creeley wrote: "I wanted the fastest juxtaposition possible, and *the least explanatory manner.*" Regarding Creeley's comment, poet John Yau writes, "The statement was made some time after Creeley saw the paintings of Jackson Pollock and other American abstract artists in Paris.... Creeley recognized that there were others who wanted to subvert their own and others' habits of thinking and seeing."[33] In his poetry, Creeley has similarly sought to challenge established modes of communication while questioning the virtue of clarity and realistic presentation. Such impulses are contrary to the "confessional" speaker, who is intimately autobiographical and thus moved to ever clearer self-examination and presentation—think of Robert Lowell's finale to his poem "Eye and Tooth": "I am tired. Everyone's tired of my turmoil."[33]

In Creeley's poems, as in the work of practically all the poets here, we find that diffusion and fragment convey an underlying perception that deep truth and centered subjectivity are *constructed* as opposed to *natural.* Perhaps no poet addresses the issue of authorial subjectivity with as much grace, wit, and sophistication as John Ashbery, so I'd like to wrap things up with a reading of his poem "Honored Guest."[34]

> Accept these nice things we have no use for:
> polished twilight, mix of clouds and sun,
> minnows in a stream. There may come a time
> we'll need them. They're yours forever,
> or another dream leaves you thirsty,
> waking. You can't see the table
> or the bread. How about a clean, unopened letter
> and the smell of toast?

School is closed today—it's thundering.
The calendar has backed up or been reversed
so the days have no least common denominator.
Anyway, it was fun, trying to figure out
who you were, what it was that led you to us.
Was it the smell of camphor? Or an ad
in an out-of-state newspaper, seeking news
of someone who disappeared long ago?
He was in uniform, and leaned against a car,
smiling at a girl who seemed to shade her eyes from him.
Can it be? Candace, was it you? There's no way
she'll look our way again.

What can I tell you? Everything's been locked up
for the night, I couldn't get it for you
if I wanted to. But there must be some way—
it's drizzling, the lamps along the path are weeping,
wanting to show you this tremendous thing,
boxed in forever, always getting closer.

This poem contains a number of the disjunctive practices typical of Ashbery, including pronominal shifts, scrambled frames of reference, and a constantly metamorphosing narrative. The title alone suggests a variety of subjects. We might imagine that the "honored guest" is the reader arriving at the text itself. The honored guest could also be a more conventional figure, say a guest in a narrative whom we expect to be fed and entertained. Both of these are plausible—sort of, but not really. It is that very inability to say for sure that something real happened to a real someone that is so wonderfully bewitching.

The first stanza introduces a plural subject—"we"—addressing the honored guest. The guest is petitioned to "accept these nice things we have no use for," an apparently self-deprecating comment that sets the reader up to expect various gracious things (say, a comforter, a tea cozy) to be presented. Instead, Ashbery undermines the reader's expectation of a generic narrative by presenting the guest with an entirely surreal amalgam of things: "polished twilight, mix of clouds and sun, / minnows in a stream." The "we" who said the useless objects had no use (objects as useless and beautiful, one might add, as a lyric poem), suddenly makes the offer conditional: "There may come a time / we'll need them," seemingly rescinding it. Then, just as suddenly, the offer is granted unconditionally again—"They're yours forever"—though the offer ultimately becomes emphatically non-utilitarian once again, replaced by "a clean, unopened letter / and the smell of toast."

Here any movement toward conclusion is continuously displaced to the point where the honored guest is left entirely with gestures toward empty space. Hunger for toast/stable meaning will not be assuaged in this poem—remember, there is only the *smell* of toast and an *unopened* letter. Instead, the reader is left with meaning in a state of suspended animation. (Again, we should remind ourselves of the non-conclusive "conclusions" of the sonnets of Bernadette Mayer, the serial poems of Fanny Howe, and the collaged texts of Lisa Jarnot).

The next stanza playfully attacks concepts of linearity with the lines: "The calendar has backed up or been reversed / so the days have no least common denominator." The possibility for the letter to be opened (meaning, made manifest) is made less and less likely here by virtue of time's own instability. Reminding us, however, that reading is fun even if it doesn't make conventional sense, Ashbery then writes: "Anyway, it was fun, trying to figure out / who you were, what it was that led you to us." Then further on, in the last four lines of the stanza, suddenly the "you" that was being addressed is pushed out of the narrative and replaced by a "He," who is leaning "against a car, / smiling at a girl who seemed to shade her eyes from him."

The first three lines of the final stanza introduce a more overt authorial persona than the one typical in Ashbery's earlier poems: "What can I tell you? Everything's been locked up / for the night, I couldn't get it for you / if I wanted to." Here Ashbery admits his inability to state an obvious truth, because meaning is "locked up" in the kind of "non-system" characterized earlier by the collapsed calendar and the shifting subjects. However, Ashbery maintains his role as lyric "teller" in the tacitly hopeless phrase, "But there must be some way—." Alluding to his romantic desire to, as Wordsworth famously put it, "see into the truth of things," Ashbery continues to insist ("but there must be some way") that he can transcribe life even as he recognizes that such a project is impossible. Ashbery's insistence that "one doesn't know anything" is in many ways illustrated by this poem. Humility in the face of the ever-escaping and tantalizing rabbit I mentioned at the beginning of this essay continues to affect Ashbery's approach in projecting and performing truth:

> it's drizzling, the lamps along the path are weeping,
> wanting to show you this tremendous thing,
> boxed in forever, always getting closer.

While one could argue that Ashbery is writing here about that old bugaboo Death, I would read the poem as talking about itself and its own desire to enact some kind of meaning or truth. Truth is in sight, "always getting closer," already upon us in the scatter of the drizzle. Again, though, Ashbery *wants* to show us this tremendous thing, but he recognizes his inability to do so—*want* implies desire as it includes lack.

In "Honored Guest," as in so many of the poems associated with the writers in this book, the "I" as transcriber of experience offers the reader a conclusion that attempts to evoke the urge toward wholeness even as it recognizes that it cannot possibly capture everything. But to fail —to not know anything—does not mean giving up. Rather, there is an even greater responsibility to continue chasing after the thought, even if it has no final, conclusive end.

As I've been arguing, investigations into what it means to be an "I" and the ability or inability of language to refer solidly and comfortingly to the things in this world continue to preoccupy not just Ashbery but all of the contemporary avant-garde. But, again, such a worthwhile and intellectually challenging agenda should not preclude the new reader from having fun. My emphasis on enjoyment is not intended to deny the difficulty inherent in these poems; in fact, the complexity is often part of the fun. Read the work of the avant-garde writers featured here (and others), and enjoy the surface surprise and music of their language. Once you've done that, you can move on to consider the vast, complex, and wonderful implications of their thinking on what it means to be you, here, thinking, feeling, and laughing.

Notes

1. Ann Lauterbach, "John Ashbery," *World Poets: Volume 1,* ed. Ron Padgett (New York: Charles Scribner's Sons, 2000), 25.

2. You may have noticed I use the word *play* a lot. Responding to my question regarding how we might teach avant-garde poets, Rae Armantrout said, "I think that to get to your question of how to encourage a reading of some of this kind of poetry, I think we have to promote the spirit of play in it." This is a wonderful introduction to what might be the guiding principle behind reading avant-garde poetry. This is not to say that the work of the writers in this book is not difficult. A lot of it is certainly dense, philosophical, and perplexing. What I'm emphasizing here, though, is to not let that difficulty put you off from enjoying the initial pleasure of the language twists, turns, and surprises that these poems offer us.

3. Many of the American avant-garde poets featured here, along with the critics who write about them, share an interest in aligning their work with the theories of post-modern and poststructuralist thinkers, among them: Roland Barthes, Michel Foucault, Julia Kristeva, Jean Baudrillard, and Jacques Derrida.

4. Walt Whitman, *Complete Poetry and Collected Prose,* ed. Justin Kaplan (New York: The Library of America, 1982), 24.

5. Ibid, 19.

6. A list or catalogue poem is any poem that itemizes things or events. You can write a poem listing all the things your cat does, for example, as Christopher Smart did in his poem *Jubilate Agno*, or you can list all the methods and ingredients for making stew, as Gary Snyder did in "How to Make Stew in the Pinacate Desert: Recipe for Locke & Drum."

7. Parataxis is the juxtaposition of clauses or phrases without the use of coordinating or subordinating conjunctions, as in: "There was snow / the postman collapsed / some say there is no meaning in a butterfly's sneeze."

8. Dickinson would prove to have a kind of delayed influence on postwar poets due to the tragic situation of her publication history. A definitive collection of her work was not available until 1955 when Thomas H. Johnson's edition of her poems were published. Earlier editions had "fixed" Dickinson's unorthodox stylistic and formal practices, essentially killing off what made her so important.

9. Susan Howe, *My Emily Dickinson* (Berkeley, Calif.: North Point Books, 1985), 11.

10. Available online at: www.centerforbookculture.org/context/no5/stein.html.

11. Charles Olson, "Projective Verse," *Selected Writings* (New York: New Directions, 1966), 17.

12. Wallace Stevens, while not as clearly influenced by Whitman and Dickinson, developed influential theories that affected the work of many American avant-garde poets considered here, especially that of the New York School.

13. Black Mountain College, founded in North Carolina in 1933, proved to be a major alternative arts center as students and professors including Charles Olson, Robert Creeley, Joel Oppenheimer, John Cage, Merce Cunningham, Robert Rauschenberg, and Buckminster Fuller gathered in a resolutely communal environment to practice their craft.

14. As Alan Golding has noted in his book *From Outlaw to Classic* (which goes into great detail about the tensions between "academic" and alternative formations in poetry), "in the early 1960s, there was "a 'cold war' (Eric Torgersen's term) between two competing anthologies: the 'cooked' *New Poets of England and America* (1957) and the 'raw' *New American Poetry*" (Golding, 28). For more information on New Criticism both as a historical movement and as a prescriptive school of thought, read Golding's book as well as Michael Davidson's *The San Francisco Renaissance* and Jed Rasula's *The American Poetry Wax Museum*.

15. Kenneth Koch, "Fresh Air," *The New American Poetry,* ed. Donald Allen (New York: Grove Press, 1960), 226.

16. Amiri Baraka, *The Autobiography of LeRoi Jones / Amiri Baraka* (New York: Freundlich Books, 1984), 232–33.

17. Quoted in Daniel Kane, *All Poets Welcome: The Lower East Side Poetry Scene in the 1960s* (Berkeley: University of California Press, 2003), 8–9.

18. George Gordon Byron, *Byron's Poetry,* ed. Frank D. McConnell (New York: Norton, 1978), 188–89.

19. Langston Hughes, "The Weary Blues," *The Norton Anthology of African-American Literature,* eds. Henry Louis Gates and Nellie Y. McKay (New York: Norton, 1997), 1257.

20. Rae Armantrout, "Anti Short-Story," *Veil: New and Selected Poems* (Middletown, Conn.: Wesleyan University Press, 2001), 12.

21. Lewis Warsh, *The Origin of the World* (Berkeley, Calif.: Creative Arts Book Company, 2001), 37.

22. Edward Lear, "There Was an Old Man with a Beard," *The Norton Anthology of Poetry*, eds. Margaret Ferguson, Mary Jo Salter, and Jon Stallworthy, 4th edition (New York: Norton & Company, 1996), 942.

23. Lewis Carroll, "Jabberwocky," *The Norton Anthology of Poetry*, 1033.

24. Alex Preminger, T. V. F. Brogan, Frank J. Warnke, et al, eds., *The New Princeton Encyclopedia of Poetry and Poetics* (Princeton, N.J.: Princeton University Press, 1993), 42.

25. Edna St. Vincent Millay, "Spring," *The Norton Anthology of Poetry*, 1273.

26. Hart Crane, *The Bridge* (New York: Liveright, 1970), 1.

27. We should note that Ashbery also writes centos. "The word *cento* comes from the Latin word meaning 'patchwork,' as in 'patchwork quilt.' The cento is a poem made entirely of pieces from poems by other authors." Ron Padgett, ed., *Handbook of Poetic Forms* (New York: Teachers & Writers Collaborative, 1987), 40.

28. Ottava rima is the name given to a stanza of eight lines of heroic verse. There are three rhymes featured in the stanza, the first six lines rhyming alternately and the last two forming a couplet. Additional examples of ottava rima can be found in Keats's "Isabella" and Shelley's "The Witch of Atlas."

29. *The New Princeton Encyclopedia,* 781.

30. Fanny Howe, "Artobiography." *Writing/Talks,* ed. Bob Perelman (Carbondale: Southern Illinois University Press, 1985), 193.

31. Harryette Mullen, *Sleeping with the Dictionary* (Berkeley: University of California Press, 2002), 23.

32. John Yau, "Beware the Lady: New Paintings and Works on Paper by Susan Bee." Electronic Poetry Center. http://epc.buffalo.edu/authors/bee/reviews/yau.html.

33. Robert Lowell, "Eye and Tooth," *Life Studies and For the Union Dead* (New York: The Noonday Press, 1964), 19.

34. John Ashbery, "Honored Guest," *Your Name Here* (New York: Farrar, Straus and Giroux, 2000), 91.

John Ashbery

ght got combed out;

t was like a field,
s, and you can feel it for mi

m on a thin vertical path,
—what?—some flower so

john ashbery

was born in 1927 in Rochester, New York, and grew up on a farm thirty miles away in a town called Sodus. After graduating from Deerfield Academy, Ashbery attended Harvard University, where he met poets Kenneth Koch and Frank O'Hara. The three poets formed the core of what has since become known as the "New York School." The trio became legendary not only for their poetry but for their wit, party going, and their collaborations with visual artists such as Larry Rivers and Jane Freilicher. After receiving his B.A. from Harvard in 1949—he wrote his senior honors thesis on the poetry of W. H. Auden, who would later name him winner of the Yale Younger Poets competition—Ashbery went on to graduate school at Columbia and New York University.

Ashbery dropped out of graduate school to work in publishing, from 1951 to 1955. A significant break occurred in 1955, when he received a Fulbright grant to study French literature in Paris. Ashbery fell in love with France and was to live there for the next ten years, working as an art critic for the *New York Herald Tribune, Art International,* and *Art News,* editing *Art & Literature* and co-editing *Locus Solus,* and writing his second book, *The Tennis Court Oath.* Ashbery returned to the United States in the mid-1960s and continued writing and working in the arts field. 1976 was a banner year for Ashbery. He received the literary equivalent of a triple crown, winning the National Book Critics Circle Award, the Pulitzer Prize, and the National Book Award for *Self-Portrait in a Convex Mirror.* This event marked Ashbery's shift from his position as a "poet's poet" to international poetry stardom, as it were, so you'll almost certainly want to read this book to see what all the fuss was about. In 1990, Ashbery was named Charles P. Stevenson Jr. Professor of Languages and Literature at Bard College, where he continues to teach.

If you're new to Ashbery's work, it might help to think about his role as a New York School poet. Read his poems alongside the work of other writers associated with the group: Frank O'Hara, Barbara Guest, Kenneth Koch, and James Schuyler. Note their predilection for a kind of deep and urbane wit, their love of comic strips and the visual arts generally, their collaborations, and their writings in other genres including novels, plays, and librettos. Ashbery and his friends were avid readers of early twentieth-century French writers such as Raymond Roussel, Guillaume Apollinaire, and Max Jacob, so you should check out some of their work as well and note how their experiments with form and their tendency toward what's known as "surrealism" has found its way into Ashbery's own work. Ashbery has also credited Gertrude Stein as an influence, and in his book *Other Traditions* (Harvard University Press, 2000), he discusses other writers who have affected the way he writes, including David Schubert and Laura Riding. Throughout his writing life Ashbery has been interested in formal innovation. Particular illustrations of this interest include *Shadow Train* (Viking, 1981), a book-length series of sixteen-line poems; *The Vermont Notebook* (Granary Books/Z Press, 2001), a catalogue of various types of Northeast Americana illustrated by the artist Joe Brainard; and *The Tennis Court Oath* (reprint edition, University Press of New England, 1997), an early collection of language experiments that are jarring in their resistance to conventional sense. Ashbery is also well known for his long poems, especially *Flow Chart* (Farrar, Straus and Giroux, 1992), a sprawling 216-page "chart" of the mind at work, and, more recently, *Girls on the Run* (Farrar, Straus and Giroux, 1999), a poem based on the posthumously discovered artwork of Henry Darger, who created a childlike fantasy world populated by little girls, demons, and evil humans.

It's really hard to say where a new reader of Ashbery's work should begin, as he's written more than twenty books of poetry—not to mention novels and collaborations with poets and artists including James Schuyler and Joe Brainard. I would suggest that you start off with *The Mooring of Starting Out* (Ecco Press, 1997), which collects Ashbery's first five books of poetry in one neat volume. It will give you a sense of the types of themes that occur in Ashbery's work today. Then see if you can get through some of his longer poems, including *Flow Chart* and *Girls on the Run*. Once you've done that, you will find it hard to stop yourself from dipping in and out of Ashbery's books generally.

[What Is Poetry]

The medieval town, with frieze
Of boy scouts from Nagoya? The snow

That came when we wanted it to snow?
Beautiful images? Trying to avoid

Ideas, as in this poem? But we
Go back to them as to a wife, leaving

The mistress we desire? Now they
Will have to believe it

As we believed it. In school
All the thought got combed out:

What was left was like a field.
Shut your eyes, and you can feel it for miles around.

Now open them on a thin vertical path.
It might give us—what?—some flowers soon?

Daniel Kane: What kinds of poetry were you taught in high school? Was all the thought really combed out?

John Ashbery: When I was a teenager, which was in the early 1940s, the high school English textbooks that we had stopped with Robert Frost, as far as modern poetry was concerned. I had to look elsewhere to find modern poets that really interested me, though at the time Frost really did. I received as a prize in high school, a Louis Untermeyer anthology of twentieth-century modern British and American poetry. There I discovered poets such as W. H. Auden, Dylan Thomas, and Wallace Stevens, whom I immediately began to read with great enjoyment. I found more of their poetry in the library, and from then on read as much contemporary poetry as I could get my hands on.

DK: It's interesting to me that you started reading contemporary poetry first—maybe teachers should start with contemporary work as an introduction to poetry?

JA: I think that is the way one should begin. I read a lot of old-fashioned poetry when I was a child, chestnuts by Tennyson, Browning, and Rossetti—all their easier works. I enjoyed these, but they didn't make me particularly want to write poetry. It wasn't until I discovered the experimenting one could do with language in contemporary poetry that I began to want to emulate these modern poets. It all seemed very difficult to me when I first began reading it, especially Stevens, as it would to just about everybody when they first encounter modern poetry. My poetry now, too! It was fun working one's way into it, and trying to puzzle it all out, like mazes and mysteries.

DK: At least Wallace Stevens provides young readers with images like people dancing around jars on top of hills in Tennessee. This might be a way to get into such poetry—enjoying this surface-level fun. Who was your favorite high school teacher? What did he or she do with poetry that you remember best?

JA: Well, I had a very nice teacher whose name was Miss Klumpp. She was helpful in getting me a little beyond the poetry in our textbook. My parents also happened to know a professor of literature at the University of Rochester, where my grandfather had been a professor. Her name was Katherine Koller. She first advised me that I should read a lot of Auden, so I did. I didn't really understand Auden much before then, although today he seems not to present that much difficulty in comparison with Stevens, for example. Auden's early poetry is much more obscure than his later poetry. I think he more or less disowned his early poetry, which was about all he'd written when I began reading him. I've always been grateful to this professor for taking the time to kind of show me around the great twentieth-century poets of the period.

DK: In "What Is Poetry" you write, "Trying to avoid / Ideas, as in this poem." Is it possible to avoid ideas in poetry?

JA: When one goes at ideas directly, with hammer and tongs as it were, ideas tend to elude one in a poem. I think they only come back in when one pretends not to be paying any attention to them, like a cat that will rub against your leg.

DK: This makes me think about some student poetry I've read, in which students decide before they have put pens to paper that they will absolutely write poems about, say, their fathers hitting them on the head. The results are often rather predictable narrative poems that describe what happened and petition the reader to feel a certain emotion. I like your idea of beginning a poem without really knowing what's going to come out of it.

JA: Also, if you write about your father hitting you on the head, you're up against a lot of competition with people who are writing about exactly the same experience. I used to tell students not to use certain subjects they seemed to gravitate to almost automatically at their age, such as the death of their grandparents—grandparents tend to die when you're in high school or college. I at least want to read about something I don't already know about.

DK: Can you tell us a little bit about the writing process behind "What Is Poetry"? For example, we've got a "frieze of boy scouts from Nagoya." There is also a mysterious "they" in the lines "Now they / Will have to believe it / As we believed it."

JA: In my free-associating, I suddenly remembered visiting the town of Chester, England, which has ramparts all around it. I had a very cheap ticket that had to be used up within a few days, so my friend and I ran around the ramparts of Chester to get back to the station. We bumped into a lot of foreign boy scouts, who impeded our trip. About the time I was writing this poem, I decided to go up to the top of the Empire State Building because it was a beautiful day and I hadn't done it in I don't know how long. The elevator was full of Japanese boy scouts with badges of the various cities they came from, one of them being Nagoya, a very large city in Japan. So those things got connected just because of one's automatic temptation to connect something with something else. "They / Will have to believe it / As we believed it"—at that point I switched to school, and "they" were the teachers, the authority figures. The thought got combed out at school, just as your mother used to comb your hair in the morning when you were running to catch the school bus. The teachers tried to make everything simple and understandable, by combing out the snarls in one's thinking.

DK: I'm glad you told us about the medieval town with the frieze of boy scouts from Nagoya, because learning that you basically made this image up out of a variety of events lets people know that they can make things up in poetry. This way, one knows one doesn't have to rely on fact all the time.

JA: I hope students already know that!

DK: I'm not so sure a lot of students do think that way. I remember having writing teachers insist, "Write what you know!"

JA: But one doesn't know anything! That's the problem.

DK: Yes, that is the problem. I think orders like "Write what you know" get interpreted to mean "Write only what you've actually experienced in real life in real time." It's nice to know from you that we can pick and choose among time, history, and imagination so that we can write a poem that sounds good and feels good.

JA: Well, I think one can, though not everybody would agree.

DK: If a teacher stopped you on the street one day and said, "Mr. Ashbery, whether you like it or not, I'm going to assign 'What Is Poetry' to my high school students and tell them to write variations on it—help me find a way to do this," what would you say?

JA: I'd like to have a teacher assign a poem that would be variations on one of my poems. There would be no recipe for doing this—just free associating, which is basically what I'm doing when I write. I use the poem as a sort of launching pad for free associations.

DK: Can people still write about flowers without sounding flowery about it?

JA: I don't think there are any things that can't be written about in poetry—it all depends on how it's done. I don't know if I've succeeded in "What Is Poetry" in taking the curse off flowers. In fact, everybody likes flowers. Why not bring them into the room with the poem? That particular line "It might give us—what?—some flowers soon?" was something I overheard someone saying. I frequently incorporate overheard speech, which there's a lot of in New York City, much of which obviously doesn't make very much sense when overheard. But it obviously makes a lot of sense to the people who are talking. I overheard a boy saying that particular line to a girl in Brentano's bookshop where I was browsing. The "thin vertical path" would be what suddenly appeared in your eyes as you open them after looking at a broad field, and the line would be perhaps a trellis or the field about to flatten out again and burst into bloom. I also like it that the couple who were talking seemed to be lovers, so the line "It might give us—what?—some flowers soon?" seemed to have special meaning for them.

DK: I read "the thin vertical path" as representing predictable poetry. I thought you were making a funny kind of editorial comment on poetry that gives us the obvious—the "flowers" of conventional poetry.

JA: That's okay with me. It's okay to interpret poetry in a variety of ways. In fact, that's the only way poetry is read, I think. We all interpret poetry according to what we've experienced, therefore everybody's interpretation is going to differ from everybody else's.

DK: Are there such things as wrong interpretations, or do you distinguish more along the lines of imaginative interpretations versus dull, unenthusiastic interpretations?

JA: It depends on the reader. If the reader is bored by his or her interpretation, then I suppose it would be a boring interpretation. I don't think it's a question of being right or wrong.

DK: You ended "What Is Poetry" with a question mark. Are there any virtues in ending a poem with a question mark or some other sign of indeterminacy?

JA: I don't know that I would say there's a virtue connected with it, or that one should set out to end a poem with a question mark—I certainly didn't. I didn't know how it was going to end—I never do. But the question mark leaves things up in the air, as opposed to slamming the book shut and ending with an "experience" of the poem. I don't know whether I do it a great deal. I once read a poem by the nineteenth-century German poet Hölderlin which ended with a comma. I thought that was a good idea, and I immediately stole it. The Hölderlin poem is in a collection called *Hymns and Fragments,* translated by Richard Sieburth.

DK: Is there anything you want to add to our discussion of "What Is Poetry"?

JA: I wrote this poem and another one called "And 'Ut Pictura Poesis Is Her Name,'" both of which deal in a playful way with the nature of poetry. Right after I began teaching, when I was in my late forties, I wasn't used to students asking me "Why is this a poem?" or "Why isn't this a poem?" or "What are poems?" I never really thought about it—I'd just been writing poems all these years. So, from thinking about the nature of poetry came this admittedly slight and light partial answer to the question, "What is poetry?"

Rae Armantrout

We get up to investigate. I

fake repairman. "I just cam

it out," he lies. "And have

indignant.

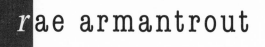

rae armantrout

was born in Vallejo, California, in 1947. Her father was a chief in the U.S. Navy, and her mother was a candy store manager. She received a B.A. in 1970 from the University of California, Berkeley, a school at the epicenter of the revolutionary excitement of the late 1960s, and then an M.A. in Creative Writing from San Francisco State College in 1975. She is currently a lecturer at the University of California, San Diego.

During the 1970s, Armantrout became associated with the West Coast branch of what is variously known as the "Language school" or "Language writing" community. In reading Armantrout, one might want to consider this fact and read her work in company of other Language-affiliated writers from this circle, such as Lyn Hejinian, Ron Silliman, Carla Harryman, and Bob Perelman. Some common approaches toward writing that might generally (if reductively) be said to be "typical" of Language poets are: examining the relationship between language and stable reference; questioning the author-centered model of composition through strategies including collaborative writing (Armantrout's *Veil* contains an extended collaboration in prose poetry with Silliman, for example); exploring the relationship between formal technique and politics; and, as Armantrout stated in our interview, displaying a "sense that poetry can be fun, and it can be heard—to be read aloud." We can distinguish Armantrout from other Language writers by noting that she tends to write in shorter forms than many of her peers and is less interested in separating language from experience.

If you're new to Armantrout's work, it's probably a good idea to start off with her book *Veil: New and Selected Poems* (Wesleyan University Press, 2001). The book will give you a good overview of her writing, with great selections from practically every book she's written. Other books that you might then want to read through include *Extremities* (The Figures, 1978), *The Invention of Hunger* (Tuumba, 1979), *Necromance* (Sun & Moon Press, 1991), and *Made to Seem* (Sun & Moon Press, 1995).

[Wake Up]

Imagine that dorm kid's confusion when I'm yelling from the
closet, "It's Jeff's dad; let me out."

               *

I get up. Our dead cat's standing by the door. I pull
off some gray threads of fur to convince Chuck something's
wrong, but what I show him looks like limp grain.
Like wild oats?

               *

We get up to investigate. In the kitchen we catch a
fake repairman. "I just came to see if you've figured
it out," he lies. "And have I?" I'm yelling, really
indignant.

[The Mix Up]

1

The pen seemed oddly juicy, nice, in what she thought of
as a dry mouth, but she was worried, either because she
shouldn't be a sucker or because she shouldn't have
sensations unexpectedly. Maybe because they shouldn't
last and what if this continued? Though now, she noticed,
worry had for some time replaced the pen.

2

Ripples are beautiful
by extension.

It's as if a series
were a stay

of execution.

Say, a list of words
starting with the letter "e":

emit, evict, evocative

     EVACULATA.

Rhapsodic to say
the birds, extending their calls,
are beginning anywhere
and adding up to zero.

3

But I want to stay because I remember when I was organizing
it all, in a frenzy really, trying to pack fear away
everywhere, so interested in the work from the date
of my first success, and now, with the effects labelled, still
not bored because I'm sure that some could be stirred up
again.

Daniel Kane: Looking at your poem "Wake Up," I see that the lines are prose-like, but the poem doesn't tell a "story" in a conventional sense. How would you justify this to a cranky student who's used to seeing lines like these used in the service of telling a traditional narrative?

Rae Armantrout: Well, these lines are snatches from dreams, from one night's dreams. I guess that's why it's called "Wake Up." To me, they do seem to have a kind of connection. For one thing, things are not what they seem in any of the sections. Identity is up for grabs. In the first section, I seem to be confused about my own identity because I'm calling myself "Jeff's dad." Jeff was a friend of my son's at the time, so why I thought I was Jeff's dad, I don't know. In the second section, I'm showing my husband pieces of my dead cat's fur. Apparently he doesn't believe that something is wrong with the cat, even though the cat is dead, so he needs this extra convincing. But when I show him the fur, it's turned into wild oats. Now wild oats, of course, has that colloquial meaning of "sowing your wild oats." That could indicate a problem in the relationship. The problem gets displaced onto the cat. That's the way dreams work—and I tend to find such displacement comic. In the third section, we get up to investigate. In the kitchen, we catch a fake repairman—maybe the repairman was going to fix these various problems.

He knows that he's not supposed to be there, he's lying about why he's there. But at this point the poem almost becomes self-referential because it's about figuring things out—figuring the dream out, figuring the poem out, or, to refer back to your question, figuring out how these things fit together. In a way, that's the job of the poem and the job of the dreamer—to figure out how things relate, how things fit together. I'm still in this accusational mode, I'm still angry, so I say: "'And have I?' I'm yelling, really indignant." Apparently I haven't figured it out, whatever it is. The fact that it is not a continuous narrative—but has various kinds of thematic connections, or imagistic connections—is pretty typical of my poetry. I'm interested in the way the mind connects things, and I think the mind connects things in many ways. I'm interested in oblique associations.

DK: I'm curious that you use the word *imagistic* in light of the fact that your conversation includes phrases like "snatches of dreams." Do you see yourself as being in the Ezra Pound/William Carlos Williams imagistic tradition, where there are a lot of juxtapositions of seemingly unrelated phenomena? I'm thinking of Pound's famous poem "In a Station of the Metro": "The apparition of these faces in the crowd / petals on a wet black bough."

RA: I think in a way I started there. Williams was the first poet I read seriously, and I really like Williams. I like Pound more for his sound—I like his prosody. That's what I started out reading. I don't mean to suggest that I am an "imagist," because I'm more interested in voice, voices that can come in. In "Wake Up" you have various voices—the repairman's voice in the dream, my voice answering him back, my voice asserting that I'm Jeff's dad, maybe Jeff's dad's voice too. I think there is more of a play of voices than you get in traditional imagist poetry, although of course Williams went way beyond imagism and used a lot of voices in his poetry, too.

DK: The Imagists never conformed precisely to the rules in the various manifesto-like statements they produced anyway!

RA: That's how it is so often with these supposed schools of poets, isn't it?

DK: In terms of the way the poem is organized, I'm curious about how you broke it up into three different sections. Did you plan on this? Does one set out before writing a poem thinking "Okay, I have these dreams, and I see it now as being in these three parts?"

RA: I do things intuitively, for the most part. This poem contains what I remember of that night's dreams, and somehow the three parts seem to me to be connected in that they were about deception, and some kind of confusion—some kind of accusation that was being hidden and repressed. I woke up, thought back over the dreams, saw a thread running through them, and then wrote them out.

DK: What's interesting to me about this poem is the sense that it is "snatches of dreams," as opposed to a neat story. A lot of writing students I've encountered are very attached to this notion of having to finish a poem. Popular music tends to underscore that narrative bias; e.g., boy meets girl, girl kisses boy, marriage, divorce, drunken solitude. Poetry such as yours offers a real alternative to those kinds of stories. How can teachers support and promote the "open" poem?

RA: As a matter of fact, the speaker in "Wake Up," who is me, is obviously wrong in the end. She's confused still. We can support the "open" or "unfinished" poem because we are still on the way, we are still trying to figure things out. We think we've come to a final answer, but we're going to find out tomorrow that we haven't. I like to dramatize that, to deliberately make the ending a kind of false bottom, where it feels like a solid ending and then you figure out that it really isn't.

DK: Can a prose poem do something more then a consciously lineated poem?

RA: In terms of not having real closure, I do that equally in my lineated poems and in my prose poems. I'm afraid I don't really have a good answer as to why I go to prose poems sometimes. I think it has more to do with the vocabulary, perhaps. In this case, there are just some pretty prosaic sentences, dialogue sentences, like "It's Jeff's dad." If I were to break that into lines, it would just seem ridiculous: "It's Jeff's / dad; / Let me / out."

DK: Prose poems are useful for less rhetorically dramatic language?

RA: I guess that's a good way to put it. In some cases, looking through some of the prose poems in *Necromance*, I saw words like *presumably* and *organization*. These are long, clunky-sounding words—essay words—that I thought would look silly in skinny little lines.

DK: That's interesting to me—in a way, the prose poem offers an approach to language that we might not ordinarily consider to be "poetic." One of the things about your poem "The Mix Up" that I'm curious about, especially considering the title, is that you are mixing up two genres: the prose poem and the lineated poem. What are the benefits of this mixture?

RA: The first section is perhaps more narrative. For instance, the last line is "Though now, she noticed, / worry had for some time replaced the pen." So it's moving in time, whereas the second section is about stopping time: "Ripples are beautiful / by extension. / It's as if the series were a stay / of execution." That "stay" is a freezing movement or moment, whereas the first and third sections are not only more narrative but they're also about an anxiety about time. There's a play here on the word *stay*. In the third section it's being used in its more colloquial sense ("I want to stay") and then in the second section it's more abstract. I guess the whole poem is about ordering, and whether things are sequential as they are in the first and third sections—or whether they can be bound into a moment, stay as they are in the second section.

DK: What happens when you hear a prose poem and when you hear these more condensed lyric lines? "The Mix Up," to me, is quite sensual, in that we have these different plays of language and hearing and tone, and different vocabularies.

RA: Now you're making me want to write more of these kinds of poems!

DK: What might you suggest are the first steps a young poet needs in order to write a prose poem? Imagine a student for whom prose is narrative, prose is essay, prose tells a story.

RA: I have my students write prose poetry. Remember, a prose poem is still a poem, and all the words require thought. You're still concerned with rhythm, you're still concerned with sound—maybe not as intensely, but you're still aware of the play of vowels and consonants—and you're still aware of the various meanings of words and the kind of play of possible metaphor and association. You still have to keep that kind of intense concentration on the small units, on the words, on the phrases, on the sentences.

DK: Are there any prose poems (not your own) that you're particularly fond of?

RA: Oh lots, lots! I love Carla Harryman's work, her book *There Never Was a Rose Without a Thorn* (published by City Lights). She never writes in verse, she always writes prose poems. One series that she has is comprised of prose poems written like the instructions for board games, but they're bizarre, surreal board games. One of them is called "Magic or Rousseau," and the pawn is Rousseau. You're moving him around this board with various philosophical options. Lyn Hejinian's book *My Life* is a classic, so is Ron Silliman's *Ketjak*.

DK: You mention writers who are considered avant-garde writers, and, by extension, difficult writers. What advice do you have for teachers out there who may be wary of teaching such poets to their students?

RA: I'm a teacher myself, and I don't think it's true that the uninitiated student *can* understand a relatively "straightforward" writer like Robert Pinsky, for instance, but *can't* understand an "avant-garde" writer like Lisa Jarnot. That isn't true—they can't understand Robert Pinsky! Poetry is very alien at first to a lot of people. What they'll "get" is really unpredictable. I'm not sure that students wouldn't "get" my poem "Wake Up." I can't promise that they would, but the chances are just as good that they would get that as they would something by Robert Pinsky. There is a lot of literary tradition and philosophical baggage that goes into reading those more mainstream poets, too, which many students now are not bringing in. If we are going to encourage more people to read avant-garde poetry, I think we have to promote the spirit of play in it. People think that the avant-garde is just all serious, grim guys marching behind Ezra Pound. But I think that if you look at some of the work of the people we've mentioned—Jarnot, Ashbery, myself, and so on—you'll see that it's very playful. There's a sense that poetry can be fun, and that it should be heard, be read aloud. I don't see why that is any more inaccessible to young people. Much avant-garde work surprises; it doesn't give you what you expect. But your basic young person has no idea what to expect, so it's all new and fresh—avant-garde or otherwise!

DK: So why are some teachers hesitant about teaching the avant-garde to their high school students?

RA: Many teachers see poetry as containing specific ingredients—deeper meanings, symbolic meanings. They can ask questions like "Here's a symbol, what does the symbol mean?" Many teachers want their students to be able to identify known literary devices and to ask how those known literary devices are working in the poem. And that's understandable, because it's something that we all know how to do—we've been trained to do that. Poetry like mine maybe doesn't contain those expected literary devices. While I think my own poetry contains a lot of metaphor, it tends to be as much anti-metaphor as metaphor. It's kind of like I'm setting two metaphors off against each other, or just seeing how far you can stretch a metaphor before it breaks.

When I teach a more experimental work, I ask the question, "What is it doing?" more than, "What does it mean?" I ask, "What patterns do you see?" I think that's a good way to begin, with anything unknown. When I give my students a text, especially a more experimental text, I start by asking, "What do you notice?" Avant-garde doesn't have to be scary; it can even be populist. Think about Ron Silliman, who would read from his book *Tjanting* in a San Francisco BART station. Nothing snobby or inaccessible about that!

Robert Creeley

No one is one
No one's alone
No world's that small
No life

You left it out

•

The shell was the

robert creeley

was born in Arlington, Massachusetts, in 1926 and grew up in rural West Acton, Massachusetts. A New Englander by birth and disposition, he has spent most of his life in other parts of the world, including Guatemala, British Columbia, France, and Spain. When Creeley was four years old, he lost his left eye as a result of earlier injuries sustained in a car accident. You'll note in the interview that Creeley credits this accident with helping him think about the nature of subjectivity and perception. In 1943 he entered Harvard (where,

coincidentally, poets Kenneth Koch, John Ashbery, and Frank O'Hara were also enrolled), but left his studies after one year to drive an ambulance in Burma. Coming of age in the years of the Second World War, Creeley feels that his world "has been one insistently involved with the unrelieved consequence of being literally human—the cultish 'existentialism' of his youth grown universal."

In the postwar years, Creeley initiated several important friendships, including one with Cid Corman, the host of a Boston radio program called *This Is Poetry*. Corman introduced him to a wider circle of working poets. He also began corresponding with William Carlos Williams, Ezra Pound, and Charles Olson (three major influences on his developing poetics). Creeley married Ann Mackinnon in 1946 and moved to New Hampshire to run a chicken and pigeon farm. The farm failed, but in 1954 Olson invited Creeley to teach at Black Mountain College in North Carolina and to edit the *Black Mountain Review*. Black Mountain, founded in in 1933, proved to be a major alternative arts center as students and professors (including Dan Rice, Joel Oppenheimer, John Cage, Merce Cunningham, Robert Rauschenberg, and Buckminster Fuller) gathered in a resolutely communal environment to practice their craft.

After Black Mountain, Creeley and his family moved to southern France and then to the Spanish island of Majorca, where he became editor of Divers Press and continued editing *Black Mountain Review*. Returning to the United States, Creeley received an M.A. from the University of New Mexico and took a teaching post there. He's been a great teacher ever since, for the most part at the State University of New York at Buffalo, where he still works.

Creeley has championed and published work by many poets associated with the Black Mountain School, including Charles Olson, John Wieners, Cid Corman, Joel Oppenheimer, Ed Dorn, Robert Duncan, Denise Levertov, and Paul Blackburn. Reading these writers' work will really help you appreciate Creeley's poetry. Olson in particular was to have an especially fruitful relationship with Creeley, as can be seen in reading the published letters between the two men. Indeed, in Olson's noted essay "Projective Verse" (1950), he quotes Creeley's slogan: "Form is never more than an extension of content." This deceptively simple idea was to have a huge influence on postwar American experimental poetry. You might also want to consider the influence of jazz on Creeley's poetics, especially that of musicians associated with be-bop, e.g., Charlie Parker, Miles Davis, and Dizzy Gillespie. As Creeley stated in our interview, "Jazz gave me an ideal sense of the possibilities of improvisation within an often very simple pattern."

Creeley has published more than sixty books of poetry in the United States and abroad. *The Collected Poems of Robert Creeley* (University of California Press, 1982) covers a thirty-year period through 1975; more recent collections include *Just In Time: Poems 1984–1994* (New Directions, 2001), *Life & Death* (New Directions, 1998), and a more inclusive *Selected Poems* (University of California Press, 1991). Creeley has also written many books of prose, essays, and interviews. If you're new to Creeley's work, I would recommend beginning with *For Love: Poems 1950–1960* (Scribners, 1962)—I'll never forget reading that book! The poems in it are especially great for anyone in love, out of love, or looking for love. Indeed, it was the first book of poetry that made me laugh and feel like crying at the same time, and it also made me want to memorize as many poems in it as possible. I remember memorizing Creeley's poems "If You" and "The Gift" and reading them aloud one Vermont night to a beautiful woman I had a crush on at the time. Since we were both only eighteen years old, such an act did not seem embarrassing and indeed she deigned to kiss me that very evening. Thanks a lot, Robert Creeley!

[*from* **Histoire de Florida**]

What was resistance.
How come to this.
Wasn't body's package
obvious limit,

could I fly,
could I settle,
could I even
be I…

And for what want,
watching man die
on tv in Holland, wife
sitting by.

She said, "He's
going off alone
for the first time
in our lives."

He told her,
"to the stars, to the
Milky Way,"
relaxed, and was gone.

What is Florida
to me or me
to Florida except
so defined.

     *

You've left a lot out
Being in doubt

you left
it out

Your mother
Aunt Bernice
in Nokomis
to the west

and south (?)
in trailer park
Dead now for years
as one says

You've left
them out
David
your son

Your friend
John
You've left
them out

You thought
you were writing
about
what you felt

You've left it out
Your love
your life
your home

your wife
You've
left her
out

No one is one
No one's alone
No world's that small
No life

You left it out

[interview]

Daniel Kane: One of the things that surprised me in *Life & Death* was your frequent use of a relatively long line. Your work has, for many years now, been characterized by a short line featuring strong enjambment—the selection above from your long poem "Histoire de Florida" is an example. Since I've heard you read a number of times, I've noticed you really emphasize your short line breaks so that the poem on the page becomes a deliberate, oddly halting, and yet insistent physical voice in the ear. Did the longer line in your recent poems come about in a way that surprised you, and what do these long lines say about your poetic voice?

Robert Creeley: They say a lot about the pace I now find most comfortable—tacitly one more reflective, less pressured by immediate feelings, more working its way along. A longer line slows things down in much the same sense that I am slowed down now by the fact of age. You probably know that William Carlos Williams's triadic line gave him useful location and resource in his old age. It offered determined "handholds" as he made his way through the pattern of sounds and rhythms otherwise possible. So I didn't think to move in these longer lines, particularly. They occurred as I wrote, proving the most viable and resourceful measure for what I was doing.

DK: Issues specific to mortality seem to rise to the surface in many of the poems in *Life & Death*. In a section of "Histoire de Florida," you write, "Old persons swinging their canted metal detectors, / beach's either end out of sight beyond the cement block highrises, / occasional cars drifting by in the lanes provided." I'm curious whether you wrote these long loping lines to suggest a kind of final inventory before death. I ask this because there's a terrific scene from Wim Wenders's movie *Wings of Desire* in which a poor fellow, knocked off his motorcycle by a speeding car, begins to list all kinds of things he sees, along with authors, foods, and so on.

RC: I don't recall any such specific preoccupation. Where I am is at the Atlantic Center for the Arts in Florida, with a company of ten other poets, each of us writing a block of whatever each day, for the mutual pile to be got to the next day. This prospect, like they say, is the beach at New Smyrna Beach, the comfortably common beach, where one sees everyone from local surfers to the people coming south for the winter. In this section I very much wanted a gathering rhythm—the "long loping lines" you noted—and you'll see that each verse is seven lines and there are four in all, making a kind of loop, or continuum—a form that has been central for me pretty much since an earlier sequence I wrote called "Helsinki Window." Life's at a stasis, so to speak. I need a form to deal with that fact. This whole poem is much involved with classic memory, from echoes of what I held to in youth as Stevens—and also Yeats, Pound, Chaucer, Wordsworth, Shakespeare, etc., etc. There are many echoes here and a very usual wonder as to how dying will occur and how one can admit it.

DK: In your poem "The Mirror," you write "Seeing is believing." Are you suggesting here that the physical situation is primary—that the imagination is just a temporary funhouse to entertain oneself as reality closes in?

RC: This was written in protest of the hopeless human slaughter in Rwanda. Little good it could do, but that's what "Seeing is believing" refers to. It's to the point that I saw primarily with my imagination, using the images I as all were given as well as the memories I had from World War II in Burma. I am suggesting that we, humanly, cannot deny the evidence of such a multitude of corpses, that we must admit such deaths and their waste. Because we felt ourselves to be different from these people, we paid, like they say, all too little attention. Of course, any reader will have his or her sense of the occasion, just as you have.

DK: I'm fascinated by this. Why didn't you name the place, the time?

RC: I can't now recall the name of the group that asked me and others to write something—it was to be used as part of a large public call for support. In retrospect, I don't think referring specifically to Rwanda would make the poem say more, so to speak—the context is finally a daily one for any of us. Ginsberg puts it aptly in "Laughing Gas":

> What's the use avoiding rats
> and horror, hiding from Cops
>   and dentists' drills?
>
> Somebody will invent
>   a Buchenwald next door.

DK: "The Mirror" also has the words, "a disgust for what we are." Much of your writing seems to me to walk on the tightrope of love and awe for the possibilities inherent in personal relationships on the one hand, and on the other a sense of disgust and even shame at the violence and nastiness we're capable of. I'm thinking here of your early poem "If You," in which you wrote: "A form of otherwise vicious habit / can have long ears and be called a rabbit." Is it fair to say this dilemma partly informs your poetics?

RC: I came of age in the Second World War and, being 4F, misguidedly wanted to "participate," and so joined the American Field Service. I ended up driving an ambulance in Burma—where I very quickly learned both the obvious uselessness of war and its grotesque highlighting of self-destructive human confusion. I don't think it's quite possible to realize the depth of that confusion until one is being shot at by altogether abstract agency, human or otherwise, bullets or bombs—put simply, someone is trying to kill you because he or she has been told to. It seems like the ultimate black comedy.

So I am saddened, to put it mildly, that so many years of my literal life have been witness to such repeatedly malignant acts as wars must constitute. That is the basic reason for the "sense of disgust," as you put it, "and even shame at the violence and nastiness we're capable of." Otherwise, the "vicious habit" you note in "If You" refers to a kind of rapacious sexual appetite that presumes all other humans are simply there for its use.

But trying to locate the boundaries for a poetics in a proposed dilemma of this kind, i.e., between some character of (benign) love and the other use of "love" as sexual appetite, has not been my interest. "The poet thinks with his poem" (as Williams says) far better describes what my experience as a writer (poet included) has been.

DK: Our discussion about "The Mirror" has led me back to the first time I started reading you, which was when I was just about eighteen years old and, for the first time, read through Donald Allen's anthology *The New American Poetry*. I found your poetry deeply emotional, responsive, and I don't mean to offend you—wildly sentimental. Over the years, I've been surprised by how many critics and readers situate your poetry within the context of the experimental. Do you see a tension in your writing between a sense of tradition and a poetry of rupture, disjunction, and sonic/aural experimentation?

RC: Not really—in that in each case a particular facet or content or means evident in what I've written is being emphasized. To that extent it's also being isolated from what else might be going on. I would think the most experimental instance of my poetry would be found in the form and content of my book *Pieces*, for example, and one might also use that work as fact of some of the most articulate "love poetry" I've written. One sees, as usual, what one's looking for—at least that gets the primary attention.

DK: Are you suggesting that the meaning of a poem is primarily subjective, depending on the environment and desires of the individual reader? Does this open-ended way of looking at meaning seem right to you, or is it cause for anxiety or frustration on the part of the author who "knows" what he's saying?

RC: I'd agree with Williams that "A new world is only a new mind," that what one calls "imagination" is the means by which we experience "reality," any reality. Having had one eye since the age of four, I know the world I see is not the normal one, no matter what the object of sight may be. I have no depth perception nor can I see three-dimensional images. All my sight is thus subjective, and whatever the objective image might otherwise be is so altered.

Even more to the point here is philosopher Ludwig Wittgenstein's "If you give it a meaning, it has a meaning." The "you" is anyone at all. You might not agree with my meaning or even recognize that it exists, but it is there nonetheless. A poem may well have, in Charles Olson's phrase, "some several causations"—reasons, points, purposes. There may well be a wish to say something specific, and this is certainly a familiar and valid possibility for poetry.

But poetry is also a structure of words, or better put, a construction of words. And whatever one may have meant the construction to mean or say, the experience of others will also be a large factor in the stabilization of such meaning. Wars have many meanings for those involved with them—as do poems, as do people. "Everybody's right," as Allen Ginsberg said. In any case, the author is not, presumably, only directing traffic toward a predestined meaning. What a bore that would be!

DK: I'm wondering what you might say to a teacher who wants his or her students' writing to make sense. I ask this because I recently heard from a teacher who was frustrated by what she deemed the "mechanical irrationality" of dada and surrealist-influenced writing. She wanted her students to have a message and get it across in "plain English." Your poem "The Mirror" appears to suggest an alternative model.

RC: Sad to say, I have had little to do with creative writing as a pedagogic undertaking. In the thirty-four years I've taught now at SUNY Buffalo, I can't have taught more than one or two classes of such kind. I have no messages simply contained in what I write, whatever my poems might be thought to say. "When I am in my painting," Pollock says to make clear his sense of that situation. When I am in my writing, I am delighted by the activity permitted and so fostered—and simply want to keep it going. I think poetry can convey clear information both of feelings and of acts—but that need not be its responsibility or purpose. There are so many instances to the contrary, I hardly have to recall them here—from Lewis Carroll ad infinitum. Finally, the occasion of the poem may well be Rwanda—but the subject, if such it can be called, is the fact of common indifference to the suffering of others, justified by the presumption that "we are not like them." In that sense, Rwanda is sadly just another occasion for this recognition.

DK: Getting back to questions of subjectivity and meaning, I'd like to ask you about your use of the abbreviation, "etc."—as in the your early poem, "The Dishonest Milkman" ("I see the flames, etc."). For me, the "etc." serves as a tacit acknowledgment of the reader's participation in the ongoing work of the poem. "Et cetera" keeps the possibilities of the poem—in terms of music and meaning—moving beyond the confines of the page.

RC: In the instance you are quoting, I hear "etc." as words (*et cetera*) and repeat it in the ending of the next line, making a useful and ironic couplet. I wonder that all your questions thus far have had so little to do with the sounds of words, with the play of that fact. For my company, one rule of thumb was Pound's proposal of melopoeia, phanopoeia, and logopoeia—and the *melos* or melody of poetry has much occupied me over the years. Otherwise I have thought, as you say, "extensively" about "etc."—and other things—all my life. "All the rest...." "The ten thousand things."

DK: In "Histoire de Florida," you incorporate lines of Wallace Stevens—for instance, "I placed a jar in Tennessee"—into the body of your stanzas. How has including other poets' lines in your own writing, without citing them, affected your understanding of poetic voice?

RC: It's like quoting in jazz. It lets one set an echo—tonal, rhythmic, or otherwise—quickly into the pattern. It's much like collage in visual art, for example. I was playing against the brilliantly flat abstraction of Stevens's statement—whose literal precision I'd never forgotten. Truly, if one so places "a jar in Tennessee," or in the bathtub, or in the backyard, or just in your pocket, the "jar" begins to shape "reality" in consequence, much like the Coke bottle in *The Gods Must Be Crazy*. (I wonder if the writer of that film was a Stevens afficionado!)

DK: You mention that Pound's proposal of melopoeia has preoccupied you. I often hear echoes of music when reading your poems: the gestures of Cecil Taylor or Archie Shepp in your book *Pieces,* for example, or the more discreet, gentle, and oddly disjunctive notes of Erik Satie in your book *Mirrors.* Have any musicians in particular influenced your writing, and if so, how has this manifested itself in your poetry?

RC: I think, with any of this, that one had best not be too didactic or literal. That is, I have used music as an instance or parallel rather than a prototype for what I wanted to do. Jazz gave me an ideal sense of the possibilities of improvisation within an often very simple pattern—for example, Charlie Parker's endless changes on the melody of "I Got Rhythm." Miles Davis (who I never got a chance to meet, sadly) seemed an absolute contemporary, born only a day or two after my own birthday. Cecil Taylor is a wonderful instance of crossover genius in all the terms of music, poetry, and dance. I am honored that he knew my work from way back—as I did his, from the time Steve Lacy was playing with him in Boston in the '50s.

Other defining people included Thelonious Monk, Bud Powell, Max Roach, Milt Jackson, John Coltrane, and Ornette Coleman (who told me once that Jayne Cortez got him to read my work), and on and on to a present friendship with Steve Swallow, the great bass player. Steve, drummer Chris Massey, reeds David Cast, wonderful guitarist David Torn, and I have just put out a CD called *Have We Told You All You Thought to Know?*, a recording of a live performance in Buffalo two years ago. Musicians have always been allies, and have heard me loud and clear from the beginning. Your mention of Satie is also much to the point. His "loops" were fascinating to me, as were Anton Webern's "reductions"—i.e., his interest in duration and structure—the question of how long a composition had to be to work as such. Music and poetry have the obvious parallel of being forms cut in time, of being serial patterns, consisting of sounds and rhythms in relation to time. One of my heroes is Thomas Campion, for example— who is an early, brilliant instance of this double.

DK: The music in *Life & Death* is certainly various. I was particularly moved by the section in "Histoire de Florida" where you repeat the phrases "You've left / it out" and "You've left / them out." There are so many stories and games and chants that seem to be referenced—I think of alphabet songs, Shakespeare's witches in *Macbeth* casting their spell, counting games—all of which use repetition to determine form. What is the role of repetition in your poetry?

RC: I remember when still in high school going with our class from West Acton into Boston, to see *Macbeth*—and that chant of the three witches has stayed in mind ever after. "When shall we three meet again…." Popular verse, like they say, uses repetition as a securing glue—the pattern of the blues is a useful example. Rhyme is repetition—of sounds, of rhythmic patterns, of thoughts. I often used the insistent repetition the couplet makes to bring disparate or discordant emphases together: "Bring it home to give it to you. / I have seen animals break in two." Stephen Fredman notes a conjunction between Walt Whitman and myself I would never have thought of. It's in his second book, *The Grounding of American Poetry: Charles Olson and the Emersonian Tradition*. He proposes Whitman and me as linked in our use of repetition. I was moved and delighted! Again he notes very usefully the so-called "parallelism" we both use as a means for structure.

DK: How were you introduced to poetry? Could you give us a bit of literary autobiography, mentioning some of the primary texts that turned you on to poetry?

RC: A book called *First Loves*, edited by Carmela Ciuraru, is useful not only for my information but some sixty-seven other poets' as well. My sister, four years older, was much involved with poetry and wrote it with active effect. Perhaps it was sibling rivalry that set me off. She introduced me to crucial books when I was ten or so, including poetry. Then teachers were a decisive link—as a survey done recently by the Academy of American Poets makes very clear. Teachers are the majority by far of those who bring the young to poetry. My grandmother—my mother's mother—was also a great lover of poetry and could recite it gloriously. My sister asked her once why she knew so much of it and she answered that she liked to have something in her head. As the note in *First Loves* makes clear, it was the emotional and erotic rush of poetry that first got to me—Alfred Noyes's

"The Highwayman" was the instance. I loved the weave of such feeling in the securing and locating sounds and rhythms. Eliot and Longfellow, all the same! I guess that if I needed to choose one precept that most served my senses of poetry over the years, it would be Pound's injunction: "Listen to the sound that it makes!" Whether it was James Whitcomb Riley or William Carlos Williams—that's where I always came in.

Fanny Howe

...so ...
...d call it spigot b...

(grapes on the palms o...

incorporated and diminish...
into little packages

4

*f*anny howe

was born in Buffalo, New York, in 1940. She grew up in an artistic and intellectual milieu: her mother was a playwright and actress, and her father was a law professor. Howe's sister (Susan) also became a major poet. Fanny Howe attended Stanford, and—like many poets in this book—has held teaching positions at a number of universities, most recently at the University of California, San Diego. Howe currently lives and writes in Massachusetts.

It's hard to associate Howe with a given "school," as her work really resists classification. However, a number of writers associated with Language poetry credit her as a colleague and influence, so it might be useful to read poets such as Lyn Hejinian, Rae Armantrout, and Susan Howe at the same time you read Fanny's work. The poet who has influenced Howe the most is probably Emily Dickinson; I've always thought Howe has more in common with this nineteenth-century renegade than she does with any other poet writing today. You'll detect this influence right away in Howe's distinctive use of em-dashes and elliptical, disjunctive phrases.

Equally renowned as poet and prose writer, Howe's writing takes on matters of social justice and the recognition of spirit, among many other themes, without displaying an impulse for polemics. Howe's poetry favors a kind of extended short form that builds longer poems out of runs of short lyrics—there are often just a handful of lines on each page, though Howe does take on denser shapes as well. Howe's *Selected Poems* (University of California Press, 2000) contains sixteen of these serial poems and reorders them without section titles to create an entirely new book. She is deeply concerned with spiritual questions, and some of her poems directly engage with a God, but with a degree of skeptical clarity that grounds the speaker while exploring the nature and difficulty of transcendence. Her collection *One Crossed Out* (Graywolf, 1997) mixes prose and poetry to represent the interior life of a homeless woman, as she tracks her consciousness through the confines of public invisibility. Hallmarks of Howe's work are her willingness to tackle subject matter that many poets avoid—and the intense care she takes—and her refusal to sacrifice complexity for a clean story.

If you are new to Howe's work, I suggest starting off with her *Selected Poems*. Other books of poetry include *Introduction to the World* (The Figures, 1986), *The End* (Littoral, 1992), and *Forged* (Post-Apollo Press, 1999). Howe has two books forthcoming from University of California Press: *Gone* (poems) and *The Wedding Dress* (essays).

[*from* **Q**]

Creation was the end that preceded means

Rain steamed on evergreens and ferns
in a larger darkness
than anyone could witness

A boy emerged from a cocoon
crying I have no right to be here!

Temperate gales blew from the jets
at Heathrow
where a baby was yelling so wide
you could see the typhus in his throat

You could also see a tall waterfall
and call it spigot because your eyes

(grapes on the palms of a saint's hands)

incorporated and diminished images
into little packages

Daniel Kane: Individual poems in your recent *Selected Poems* are untitled, though you do have titles for groups of poems. This makes me think of your work as "serial poetry." How would you define a serial poem in your own terms, and what does a poem gain by lacking a title?

Fanny Howe: The term "serial poem" has always seemed artificial to me, although I know what you mean by it. The fact is, I don't even like "modernism" or "material text" or any term that tries to surround an action that is simultaneously trying to be free. So this leads directly to my problem with titles, because (to me) they put a lid on the loneliness of the poem. And they influence the way it is read. Freedom at any cost!

Because titles come after the composition of the poem, they are not usually part of its eruption. They have a kind of leaden quality, unless they are like song titles that are lifted from inside the song itself, or are muted mood messages, and are not music, the way titles are also words. I tend to scribble down the messages as they come in, and then elucidate and organize them into a cluster based on the time zone surrounding their arrival. I think of them as days more than anything else, days in the ancient sense of an act or a feeling that begins and completes itself. How many times the sun rises and sets in that kind of day is of no importance. All that matters is knowing when it ended, and, more mysteriously, when it began.

DK: I found the poems represented under the title *Q* particularly moving and interesting. They strike me as a narrative of travel—from one physical location to another, from one political awareness to another, and from one emotional condition to another. Did you write this series during a particularly peripatetic period in your life?

FH: *Q* was written in an intense period of uprootedness that was a more exaggerated version of the one I had experienced for twenty years and longer. I don't know what's wrong with me, but I can't get settled. It is deeply unpleasant, especially because my family isn't traveling with me anymore. *Q* was part of the two-year period I spent working in London, seven years ago. I had to travel by train, constantly, as part of the job, and stay in dismal B & B's in the outskirts of small cities. Trains made me happy by contrast, and even now I feel most at rest in motion.

DK: In the poem from *Q* that begins "Creation was the end that preceded means," you write:

> Rain streamed on evergreen and ferns
> in a larger darkness
> than anyone could witness
>
> A boy emerged from a cocoon
> crying I have no right to be here!

I'm interested in the lack of punctuation in your poems. The open-endedness such a lack evokes seems particularly suited to the travel narrative.

FH: I think for me poems are sentences, which may be why they are getting shorter. I love a complete sentence, and all that it contains in the way of balance and aspiration. I love prose sentences. But a whole poem of mine is a sentence composed of sound-lines (bars), each line being the equivalent of a complex word. Each sound-line floats in tandem with the next one. Each one is a word. The group of sound-lines or words forms a sort of sentence which is a poem.

A few words create together one word, and that word is on a line, and the next line consists of another long word made up of words. Then the poem is composed of both many and few words. The lines themselves demonstrate their separateness and, at the same time, the gravitational pull in relation to each other.

Prose only differs to the extent that the lines jump on each other, left to right, instead of falling down from an upwards position. The jumping to the side saves paper (time and space), but it also indicates another thought process—one with a goal. It's the difference between taking a walk and sitting still. Prose has just as much poetry in it as a poem does. It's just in a rush to get somewhere and bears more guilt, always trying to justify itself.

DK: What are the advantages of writing lines as "the equivalent of a complex word"?

FH: Such an approach offers a kind of cubist, or three-dimensional, look at language. By stacking the independent clauses and keeping them as free as possible from the chaining effect of the next lines, the words create an optical illusion of depth and clamor. The line stands alone, and in tandem, and in space.

DK: In the poem we've been discussing, you write:

> your eyes
>
> (grapes on the palms of a saint's hands)
>
> incorporated and diminished images
> into little packages.

Are you critiquing the role of the image in poetry?

FH: No, I was literally thinking of the way sight works—by glimpse and association—and the saint who blinded herself rather than get married held her eyes on the palms of her hands like an offering of grapes. Her eyes, usually the containers of images, became two things preceding images.

DK: Who was this saint? Is she a model for your own independent poetics?

FH: St. Lucy of Syracuse refused to marry a man who then was infuriated when she gave all her dowry away to the poor. He had her arrested, but her body was so inert she couldn't be moved. She is represented, often, with the balls of her eyes in a dish or in her hands. I don't really know if she did it to herself, or if someone else blinded her. The story tends towards her self-blinding. This bold and agonizing action against authority—an act of pure resistance—*does* seem wonderful to me because it concerns an individual who is punished for having visions and vatic energies and who can't help herself from expressing them. I am on the side of the poets who write from that perilous point: John Wieners, Alice Notley, Bernadette Mayer, Will Alexander. It may be generational. It seems old-fashioned.

DK: I like it that you're old-fashioned! Romanticism lives! The "grapes on the palms of a saint's hands" is certainly a surprising image. It is a kind of oracular intervention into a poem about dailiness. The saint reminds me of the lyric's place in mystical and religious history. Do you conceive of your role as poet in such magical terms?

FH: Orpheus is everywhere. So is religion as an Orphic presence. Maybe it isn't necessary to think in terms of the lyric. What I do every day comes from one impulse, whether it's writing or washing—to convert, to be wholehearted, happy, brave, faithful, without a doubt. Contradiction has gotten me the closest to this experience. Nothing works and everything works. Creation was the end that preceded means. I think we may have everything backwards, literally everything! And eyes are the evidence.

DK: You mentioned cubism in the context of your writing. How has the work of Gertrude Stein influenced your poetics?

FH: This question leads to the matter of lineage, which has been tackled recently and eloquently by Leslie Scalapino. I think she and I may share a doubt about placing work in relation to a literary work before it, partly because there is no such thing as before, if you really think about it. And also because the preservation of hierarchies seems to accompany any discussion of lineage. We see the containment of "literature" in a corral, segregated from all the other milieus in which we develop.

DK: In spite of your hesitation with respect to lineage, I'm going to insist that you tell us who you'd like to see yourself in company with and which poets most influenced you when you were growing up.

FH: Well, first there was Shakespeare. Then there was Keats. And then there was a little anthology, *World Poetry* by Oscar Williams. I went mad for Chinese, Russian, and French poetry in translation. I went to a school that taught Latin and, of course, fussing with the *Aeneid* was a great thing. But I think it was studying French in high school, reading Charles Baudelaire, Arthur Rimbaud, and Paul Verlaine that really tipped me over. A poetry of translation, that was my original joy. Even Shakespearean was a kind of language in translation.

And so I believe that teaching by listening—without being asked to analyze lines for meaning but just being asked to hear the music of languages half-understood—is a great way to get comfortable with poetry. About twenty years ago I came across a book called *The Ghazals of Ghalib* in which several different poets translate the same poems from the same original "rough" translation. Each poet came up with a wholly separate interpretation and approach to each poem. But it was the ghazal as a way of thinking and living that really moved me. John Wieners has always been a liberating poet for me, as well.

DK: You mentioned that you rarely teach poetry. Is that a matter of choice, or do you have strong opinions about the teaching of poetry writing?

FH: I am glad I haven't been a poetry teacher often, although it wasn't a choice. I was hired at UC San Diego as a fiction writer, and it is fiction that I have taught for the past twelve years. While fiction is more demanding, in terms of the time spent on the line editing, it is pretty hardy and resilient and can take a lot of talk about it. I think poetry is less easy to take apart and put back together whole. Also, teaching itself takes its toll on writing. I really don't want to get tired of poetry, ever, or cynical about it, even at its most unformed student stage. I have become less interested in the problems of fiction, the longer I have taught it. This could have happened with poetry, but thankfully didn't.

DK: If a teacher asked you for advice on teaching the poem of yours that begins "Creation was the end that preceded means," how would you respond?

FH: I would talk about it in relation to the poems in the series called "Introduction to the World," because there the subjects of evolution and bounded time are explored a little more explicitly. When I wrote "Creation," I was reading liberation theology, which proposes a beginning and an end to the natural world, and one in which the economy of labor and spirit are inseparable.

If one thinks of the natural world as offering unlimited means for human survival, one can choose to see evolution as endlessly occurring in an open field, and all matter given to those who are the best at exploiting its uses. Alternatively, one can envision a limited opportunity, one in which the living and the dead are involved in a single inseparable struggle, mutually responsible for each other, and with the only freedom being one of spirit or of mind.

In "Creation," I wanted to take the latter position, as if to say that although the story is finished, it includes all time (ferns, planes, and people who suffered). This means we have a responsibility to the past and the future, which are neither past nor future. I would read the images as a series of signs that fell out of the first line, images of events that have a moment of freedom before they are captured and become offerings.

Lisa Jarnot

to meet him, or rather that you c

maintaining the inner truth
of the favorable outlook, like th
where Emperor Wu lives in yo
and this is dangerous— and
this is not what I ordered, or

ay that Emperor Wu lives i
hat I was a kid crossing th
where I crossed the street a
maintained the inner truth
for Emperor Wu lived in
with a heart free of preju

*l*isa jarnot

was born in Buffalo, New York, in 1967, which makes her the youngest writer featured in this book. She attended the State University of New York at Buffalo, where she studied with Robert Creeley, and received an M.F.A. in Creative Writing from Brown University. At Brown, she studied with Michael Palmer, who got her interested in the work of Robert Duncan. Jarnot has led a varied life as a pizza-maker, dishwasher, librarian, and teacher. She currently lives in Brooklyn.

Jarnot has been an active figure in the contemporary poetry scene. She co-edited *An Anthology of New (American) Poetry* (Talisman House, 1998). The reason I mention this is because checking out the poems in that book might very well help you appreciate Jarnot's work; there you will find poems by Jarnot's peers, including Jordan Davis, Peter Gizzi, Lee Ann Brown, Renee Gladman, and other younger writers who in many ways share Jarnot's aesthetics and lyrical impulse. I also urge you to read Bernadette Mayer in unison with Jarnot, as Mayer's playful, often whimsical humor combined with deep intelligence finds its way into Jarnot's work. Indeed, Jarnot told me: "Everyone said, 'You have to hang out with Bernadette because she's the coolest person in the world.' So I hung out with Bernadette and she was the coolest person in the world."

For visual counterparts to Jarnot's work, I suggest looking at Duchamp's mixed-media assemblages and Picasso's cubist paintings. Also go see any dance performance by Merce Cunningham that you can, read John Ashbery's centos, Ted Berrigan's sonnets, Frank O'Hara's poems, and the work of Beat writers Allen Ginsberg and Jack Kerouac. Listen to John Cage's music, and then play some Johnny Cash. These works' joyous weirdness, playfulness, and pleasure in response to the mixed-up accidents of the everyday have influenced Jarnot profoundly.

Since Jarnot at this point has only two full-length collection of poems, *Some Other Kind of Mission* (Burning Deck, 1996) and *Ring of Fire* (Zoland Books, 2001), you might as well treat yourself and get both books. I especially encourage you to read her work aloud, as her poems feature lots of repetition and variation, and sound great. Jarnot's biography *Robert Duncan: The Ambassador from Venus* is forthcoming from the University of California Press, so we have something to look forward to there as well.

[Emperor Wu]

Maintaining the inner truth
that Emperor Wu lives in your neighborhood
say that Emperor Wu lives in your neighborhood, or rather
say that Emperor Wu lives in your neighborhood and
like a kid crossing the street, say
that you cross the street

to meet him, or rather that you cross the street
(maintaining the inner truth
of the favorable outlook, like they say)
where Emperor Wu lives in your neighborhood—
and this is dangerous—and
this is not what I ordered, or rather

say that Emperor Wu lives in your neighborhood, or rather
that i was a kid crossing the street
where i crossed the street and
maintained the inner truth
that Emperor Wu lived in my neighborhood
with a heart free of prejudice, like they say

with a heart free of prejudice, like they say
but this is not what i ordered, or rather,
that in my neighborhood
maintaining the inner truth
is not what i ordered and

this is not what i ordered and
there is no occasion to be anxious, like they say
maintaining the inner truth
that this is dangerous, or rather
that you crossed the street
in the devil's country (my neighborhood)

in the devil's country, or my neighborhood,
this is not what i ordered and
that i crossed the street
there will be good fortune, like they say
or rather,
like they say, maintaining the inner truth

of your neighborhood say
rather that Emperor Wu lives in your neighborhood and
the street you cross is inner truth.

Daniel Kane: One could describe your book *Some Other Kind of Mission* as a book containing mostly prose poems. How do you see this poem, "Emperor Wu," fitting in to your overall plan?

Lisa Jarnot: There are a lot of pieces in *Some Other Kind of Mission* that use collage. The Emperor Wu sestina is one of these. Most of the material comes from the *I Ching*. A lot of it comes from a recording I have between Bob Dylan and an obsessed fan of his. There's also the refrain "like they say," which is a phrase Robert Creeley sometimes uses in his poems.

DK: Could you suggest some ways for students to incorporate collage techniques into their writing?

LJ: I think poems are always collage on some level. You're taking in information and you're putting it together from different sources. Sources can be as varied as something you've overheard, or something that's going on in your head. When I started writing *Some Other Kind of Mission,* I was having trouble keeping up with a daily writing practice. I started to collect pieces of paper and put them together in different ways. I did this in an effort to come up with starting points for poems. It's like a little magic trick—collage helps me see what different sources can tell me, and what direction those sources can send material in. Even though it seems random, collage helped me see how certain material might be related to my life or my personal narrative at a given point. We're surrounded by messages in the culture all the time. We're not always aware of these messages, so collage is a way to force awareness out of the random flow of information that's constantly bombarding us. A lot of the work I've done comes out of advertising, flyers off the streets or signposts. I actually physically collected a lot of these pieces of paper, which then contributed to the visual collages in the book. I'd lay these papers out on the table, and put them together like I would put together a jigsaw puzzle.

DK: You like to use repetition a lot in your work: I've noticed individual phrases and words that repeat in individual poems and throughout the book. For example, you have a poem that begins "Past noon. i look about meridians. i think up for meridians of / noon. about meridians of pushing junk. there is if there is i am / cuz the tern. and if. and if the robin's head. if noon then at / meridian." What is interesting or attractive to you about this incantation? How might students of writing pick up on this kind of practice?

LJ: I think of poetry as related to song. Repetition helps a reader read a poem rhythmically. I also think that there is a psychological construct at work. One goes through repetitions of thought neurotically, and a lot of this book tries to document that. I wanted to chart out what was happening in my head, to make a map of the mind at work. Those repetitive phrases bought me closer to writing exactly what was going on in my brain at particular moments.

DK: Your use of repetition also suggested to me a kind of avant-garde blues. Where Mississippi John Hurt might sing, "Oh lay me down a pallet on your floor / oh lay me a pallet down on your floor," you sing, "i look about meridians. i think up for meridians of noon." You've extended the blues into a neurotic suburban space.

LJ: I think that's pretty accurate. A lot of these poems were written as I was listening to music. I wrote a lot of *Some Other Kind of Mission* during a car trip with headphones on. So there was music going on, and then there was this story going through my head.

DK: Can you name some other works that employ repetition? Is there a heritage of repetition that you look to?

LJ: Christopher Smart's poem *Jubilate Agno*. From there, Walt Whitman and Allen Ginsberg. Gertrude Stein is also an influence, though she sometimes works with repetition in a less melodic way. It's as if she's using repetition to subvert a melody—it's a klunky repetition. I like John Ashbery's sestinas—his poem "The Painter" is terrific. Bernadette Mayer also uses repetition in her work in a way that's been very influential and useful to me.

DK: Are there any other "traditional" forms you can think of that can be reworked and used without sounding archaic? How can students learn about things like sonnets and sestinas without getting bored?

LJ: Sonnets—any kinds of sonnets—are great. Read Bernadette Mayer's sonnets. Read Ted Berrigan's sonnets. Mayer uses the sonnet as a space where she adheres to the traditional idea that there's going to be one statement made, with the couplet at the end that "turns" or "sums up" the statement. She really focuses on that when she writes a sonnet, yet she's writing totally contemporary sonnets, and they're fun. There are a lot of forms that come into music—villanelles, ballads. It's helpful to think of what you like in contemporary "pop" culture that contains traces of formal poetic characteristics—that way, you might be more open to learning about traditional forms.

In general, I think knowing about traditional forms is very important if you really want to be a poet. In order to be a free verse poet you really have to know traditional forms. "Free verse" doesn't mean random, open forms. It means something else is at work. It may not be meter, it may not be end-rhyme, but there is something at work that holds the poem together. A good foundation for understanding that is to know how traditional forms work.

DK: How is "Emperor Wu" an American poem?

LJ: I suppose that as a whole, *Some Other Kind of Mission* has a weird American streak in it. It's American in the sense of addressing the stereotypical notions of the individual in the landscape or in the wilderness—there's a certain lonesomeness implied.

DK: I ask you this question because I read "Emperor Wu" to a friend from England. Her immediate response to it was to exclaim, "That's so American!" She said, "English people don't think in terms of neighborhood. In London you don't ask, 'What neighborhood do you live in?'" She was pleased by this notion of people thinking of themselves as living in a community.

LJ: That's funny. I never thought of that poem as American in terms of its relationship to neighborhood. I was thinking more along the lines of the actual physical activity and environment suggested by the poem. It's a very spacious poem—kind of like "Go west, young man."

DK: The poem does suggest wide open spaces to me, though not necessarily wide open in the sense of plains or mountain ranges. I actually picture a kind of suburban landscape with detached homes, wide streets, and basketball hoops above the garage. Can you suggest a few ways students might use their own suburban landscapes as content for their poetry?

LJ: I think there are particulars one is surrounded by that can always contribute to what one does in a poem. Kids in the suburbs have great things to write about—shopping malls full of particulars. Things that appear at first to be insignificant become significant once you let them into the poem.

DK: Is there anything else you want to say to budding poets out there, many of them right now shooting hoops in suburbia?

LJ: Well, the suburbs are certainly part of my background. I think I would say that one doesn't have to depend on—or be surrounded by—high culture to be a poet. And "Emperor Wu" is a simple poem in many ways— it's mostly about a relationship between two people. You have Emperor Wu, and you have the author, whoever that is, and it's not clear what the connection is between them. It certainly has to do with childhood, figuring out that connections go in unexpected directions. That's also the idea of using the I Ching, learning ahead of time whether you're going to make a certain connection, and what direction that connection is going to go in. Ideas like "inner truth," I was just throwing that out there—I mean, what does that mean? That's why I put it in there. What could that possibly mean?

Kenneth Koch

and the snappy

e sloped marine sk

s will go on and the

n connection with yo

m

madly, will go explodi

d, planispheres, ingeniou

ds of atmospheres, unequa

l piers, fumisteries, emphat

sweets, O Peace, to you

kenneth koch

was born in Cincinnati, Ohio, in 1925. In 1943, Koch was drafted and served as a rifleman in the Pacific fighting the Japanese. (Koch would later describe his experiences in the poem "To World War II.") After the war, Koch went on to study at Harvard, where he befriended poets Frank O'Hara and John Ashbery. After graduating, Koch received a Fulbright to study in Aix-en-Provence, where, according to French Cultural Counselor Pierre Buhler, he "skipped class to frolic on the slopes of Mont Sainte-

Victoire." Koch moved to New York City in 1948 to attend Columbia University. He received his Ph.D. in 1959 and began a career there as a professor. Koch met painters and musicians who were to exert a great influence on him and make appearances in his poems, including Larry Rivers, Jane Freilicher, Alex Katz, and others. Being in New York at that moment in history when rents were cheap and the city was flooded with artists of all kinds meant that on a given night, Koch might hear Billie Holiday singing at the 5 Spot or have a drink with Jackson Pollock and Willem de Kooning at the Cedar Bar.

Koch taught at Columbia for decades, and through his popular poetry workshops influenced generations of poets. Poet Bob Holman once told me, "I was in Kenneth Koch's class in 1968, at Columbia. Koch was a brilliant teacher. He came into class on the first day, threw his arms around himself and shouted, 'Walt, I love you!' Thus began our study of U.S poetics. I'd never been on a first-name basis with a poet before, let alone a dead poet like Walt Whitman, but Kenneth was." Koch died on July 7, 2002.

If I had to assign roles to New York School writers, I'd name John Ashbery the philosopher; James Schuyler the quiet, flower-growing type; Frank O'Hara the debonair and funny artiste; and Kenneth Koch the class clown. As a poet, Koch was unique in terms of his passionate commitment to humor, but also in his abilty to combine the hilarious and fantastical with the lyrical and the beautiful, and with daily life. For example, *The Art of Love* (Random House, 1975) contains several advice poems with instructions on such things as how to make love and how to cure an octopus! Koch, of course, had a serious side as well—he was a master of poetic form, a voracious reader of literature, and exceptionally gifted in a wide range of literary genres, especially autobiographical poems and travel poems. While his tremendous energy and passion for poetry could sometimes be daunting (Frank O'Hara once wrote in a poem, "I think I am going crazy / what with my terrible hangover and the weekend coming up / at excitement-prone Kenneth Koch's"), his exuberance has given a lot of poets license to be wild and crazy in their own work—for instance, Lewis Warsh, Bernadette Mayer, and Lisa Jarnot. Other writers deeply influenced by Koch's work include Charles Bernstein, Joe Ceravolo, Ron Padgett, and Ted Berrigan—and these are just a few.

Koch's many books include *A Possible World* (Knopf, 2002); *Sun Out: Selected Poems 1952–1954* (Knopf, 2002); *New Addresses* (Knopf, 2000); *One Train* and *On the Great Atlantic Rainway: Selected Poems 1950–1988* (both Knopf, 1994). Maybe the best place to start reading Koch is with *On the Great Atlantic Rainway*. Choose your favorite poems from there, find out what books they were first published in, and then buy those books. However, I should warn you that you might fall in love with all of Koch's poems, which means you should have money stashed away somewhere so you can buy everything he's written.

You will notice many references in our interview to The Poetry Project, a reading series at St. Mark's Church in downtown New York. It's been around since 1966, and is known as a major forum for the contemporary avant-garde. Why not pay it a visit? There are readings every Monday, Wednesday, and Friday. The address is 131 E. 10th St., New York, NY 10003.

And the big boats come sailing into the harbor for peace
And the little apes are running around the jungle for peace
And the day (that is, the star of day, the sun) is shining for peace
Somewhere a moustachioed student is puzzling over the works of Raymond
     Roussel for peace
And the Mediterranean peach trees are fast asleep for peace
With their pink arms akimbo and the blue plums of Switzerland for peace
And the monkeys are climbing for coconuts and peace
The Hawaiian palm
And serpents are writhing for peace—those are snakes—
And the Alps, Mount Vesuvius, all the really big important mountains
Are rising for peace, and they're filled with rocks—surely it won't be long;
And Leonardo da Vinci's *Last Supper* is moving across the monastery wall
A few micrometers for peace, and Paolo Uccello's red horses
Are turning a little redder for peace, and the Anglo-Saxon dining hall
Begins glowing like crazy, and Beowulf, Robert E. Lee, Sir Barbarossa, and
     Baron Jeep
Are sleeping on the railways for peace and darting around the harbor
And leaping into the sailboats and the sailboats will go on
And underneath the sailboats the sea will go on and we will go on
And the birds will go on and the snappy words will go on
And the tea sky and the sloped marine sky
And the hustle of beans will go on and the unserious canoe
It will all be going on in connection with you, peace, and my poem, like a
     Cadillac of wampum
Unredeemed and flying madly, will go exploding through
New cities sweet inflated, planispheres, ingenious hair, a camera smashing
Badinage, cerebral stands of atmospheres, unequaled, dreamed of
Empeacements, candled piers, fumisteries, emphatic moods, terrestrialism's
Crackle, love's flat, sun's sweets, oh peace, to you.

Kenneth Koch: Before you got here, I was trying to think of the best poetry reading I ever heard. I was driving in from Eastern Long Island, with John Ashbery in the car, and he read me "The Skaters." That's the best poetry reading I've ever heard. The second best reading I ever heard was one that Frank O'Hara gave at some gallery—in fact, this was the first time I heard him read. He read "For the Chinese New Year & For Bill Berkson." I heard something in Frank's voice, a kind of tone that clarified something for me, so that was a terrific reading for me. Those were the two best ones I ever heard.

Daniel Kane: The first one was rather exclusive!

KK: Yes, I would say so! [*laughs*] On the whole subject of poetry readings, I must admit I'm kind of skeptical, because I'm not sure that much has ever happened because of poetry readings. I like to read poems in books. Don't you? There are very few people I like to hear read. I like to hear Ron Padgett read.

DK: I remember hearing Ann Lauterbach read before I ever read her poetry. As she was reading, her hands started moving and dancing in front of her—it seemed as if she were approximating the words visually by sculpting them in the air with her hands. I thought it was all quite thrilling. When she was done, I dashed off and bought her book *Clamor.*

KK: A reading that did have a big influence on me, I now remember, was one which was held up at Columbia University that Allen Ginsberg did, in the late 1960s, with John Hollander. It was during the Vietnam War, and I had not written a political poem since I was a teenager. I was impressed by Allen's straightforwardness, which is something I got from the reading I think even more than I could have from reading his poems on the page. In person, Allen displayed how straightforward he was about everything. He read a lot of "political" poems about the war, and I thought, "Why am I not writing about this war, which I object to so much?" And I didn't like what was happening to my students, what was happening to anybody, so I started to write my poem "The Pleasures of Peace" as a direct result of being inspired by that Ginsberg reading. I worked on this poem for more than a year, maybe two years. It was very hard for me to work on a poem about the war. You know sometimes your body rejects an artificial heart? Well, my poetry rejected everything about the war, everything that was about suffering. So it turned out to be a poem about the pleasures of the peace movement.

DK: Did you see your aesthetics, which for the most part do not include overtly political content, fitting in somehow with the political excitement going on at the time?

KK: I remember being always willing to read my poetry for what I thought was a good cause, whether or not my poetry spoke about the cause. And it usually didn't. That's about it. I was happy to read against the war even before I wrote "The Pleasures of Peace." If people wanted me to read something about roller coasters to show that poets were against the war, I would always do it. But I don't know much about the "scene" at the St. Mark's Poetry Project. I was never really a part of that scene. By the time it got to be something that I took part in with any regularity, I was already sort of an old-timer.

DK: Even though you and Ashbery and O'Hara and James Schuyler are seen, in a strange sort of way, as spiritual founding fathers of the Poetry Project?

KK: The Poetry Project didn't have anything to do with the formation of my poetry, or John's or Frank's or Jimmy's, so far as I know, though I have been inspired by reading there; I've always liked to read there. The audience is so smart. That is to say, they're smart in this particular way that they're up on what's going on in poetry. It's like being a scientist talking to other scientists, and you're excited because they have the same kind of laboratory you have. I was slightly afraid sometimes to read new work at The Poetry Project, because I was afraid things would be swiped. Everybody is on this high frequency there! I had a very funny time with Ted Berrigan about that. I read there one year—my series "In Bed," about a hundred short poems, all with "bed" in the title. So I read it at St. Mark's, and within a couple of months I got a little book from Ted Berrigan, and it had a little poem in it called "By the Seashore" or something like that. And the entire poem is "There is a crab/in my bed." And I thought, Oh shit! I didn't say anything to Ted. But I happened to be talking to Anne Waldman about something and I mentioned this to her, and she said, "Oh!" She was very happy; she would get to reproach Ted with it. But I said, "Don't tell Ted," and she said "Oh, no no no." But she couldn't help but tell Ted. And Ted wrote me a letter assuring me that this was not true, that he'd written the poem four years before my "In Bed" poems. Alice Notley later told me, "Kenneth, I know that for sure. I'm the crab!"

DK: What do you think the effect of the Donald Allen anthology, *The New American Poetry,* was on your career, especially in the way it classified you as a "New York Poet"?

KK: I have no idea. I don't even know what my career is. I got a little, tiny bit famous for writing *Wishes, Lies, and Dreams.* I got asked all around the country to talk about teaching children to write poetry, but my poetry— I don't know about my career. Poetry books in this country are sometimes reviewed and sometimes not. It's very hard to know what makes a career. The best thing that happened to me was having John Ashbery and Frank O'Hara as friends. To have two poets who delight you and scare you to death is the best thing that I ever got. I don't know what that anthology did for anyone's career. Frank's career, outside a small audience, seemed to start after his death. I don't think it did anything for my career, or Ashbery's. Ashbery's big academic career started very oddly, with *Self-Portrait in a Convex Mirror.* All that glorious early work was more or less ignored. Very strange!

DK: *The New American Poetry* certainly had an enormous effect on poets, like Berrigan and others, who looked up to you and your friends. Did you have anything consciously to do with the creation of a "second-generation" New York School?

KK: You're asking me things I don't know anything about! The New York School has always been such a shadowy thing. I was aware that there were these terrific talented kids downtown who really liked John and Frank and me and particularly liked John and Frank. I was aware of that, and then after a while it seemed that Ted Berrigan was sort of the daddy of the downtown poets, taking care of everybody and showing them what it was like to be a poet. I taught a number of those guys in various places. I taught Ron Padgett at Columbia. David Shapiro was my student, too. At the New School I had Tony Towle as a student, and Bill Berkson, and then at Wagner College even Ted came as my student. Ted pointed out to me something very interesting. He said, "Kenneth, do you know every time you mention Paul Valéry you go like this?" [*puts his right hand on top of his head*]. I thought that was very astute of him. I was very embarrassed, so I stopped doing that. Joe Ceravolo was my student at the New School. That's a pleasure for a teacher, to have a brilliant student like that who had hardly written a poem before. I decided to teach at the New School not only because I wanted a job, but I really thought I knew a secret about poetry that nobody knew except John and Frank and me. I knew about this new aesthetic, this new way to write poetry, and I wanted to spread it around, because I thought it was dumb to think that these other bad poets were writing poetry. I taught with a lot of enthusiasm. I really had a mission to make this aesthetic clear to people. I liked this idea of there being more New York poets.

DK: I notice you use the word *aesthetic* as in "I wanted to teach this aesthetic." How would you define that aesthetic?

KK: Well, let me tell you a few assignments I used at the New School. I had people read William Carlos Williams and imitate him. This was to help them get rid of meter, rhyme, and fancy subject matter. I had them use ordinary American language, spoken language. I had them write poems about their dreams. I had them write stream-of-consciousness—this was to get their unconscious stuff into their poetry. I had everybody write short plays, prose poems, transform an article in a newspaper into a poem, and I had them write sestinas. I wanted my students to break away from "poetry" poetry. This was something I thought was French. I was very influenced by Max Jacob. Do you know his work? You should read him. From Jacob I learned how to be comic and lyrical at the same time. That was quite a discovery. It helped the determination to get rid of Eliot, and depression, and despair, and inky-dinky meter. I read a critic that I make fun of in my poem "Fresh Air" who said that iambic pentameter was the only "honest" English meter. So, getting back to your question of what is the New York School aesthetic—I don't know, just a lot of fresh air, to have fun with poetry, to use the unconscious, to use the spoken language, to pay attention to the surface of the language.

DK: Your poem "Fresh Air" seems to have set up a distinction between so-called "avant-garde" or "outsider" poetry and academic poetry. What is academic poetry?

KK: It changes. The academic poetry I was ridiculing then has mainly—but not entirely—gone away. Now there are new kinds of bad poetry that you could call "academic." The kind in "Fresh Air" is by now old-fashioned, like iceboxes—the new kinds of academic poetry are like bad refrigerators. The academic poetry that I made fun of in "Fresh Air" had a heavy dose of myth. It was all these American poets of the '40s and '50s who had gone through their Yeats shots and Eliot shots, and they all had the fever of the bone, the skeleton, Odysseus, all that stuff. Now it's funny what academic poetry has turned into. I've always wanted to write more poems like "Fresh Air," but I didn't have the incentive. After a while, there didn't seem to be a discernible enemy. There were too many enemies. But bad poetry never goes away. Then there was this whole period—it's still with us, I think—of the whole "workshop" kind of poem. "Grandpa dies on the way to the garage," or "I'm having a love affair with a student," or something. At the time I wrote "Fresh Air," academic poetry was the poetry that was in Donald Hall, Robert Pack, and Louis Simpson's book *New British and American Poets*. It was Snodgrass, Ciardi…. That anthology was one of my major inspirations for writing my poem "Fresh Air." That's where I got the idea that all this poetry was about the myth, the missus, and the mid-terms.

DK: Donald Allen stated that all the poets in *The New American Poetry* shared a common debt to Pound and Williams. Why was Pound acceptable to so many of the avant-garde poets, whereas Eliot, especially the later Eliot, wasn't?

KK: Particularly in *The Cantos,* when they're good, Pound has this very quirky way of talking, very conversational. He gives you all these pleasures—a very flat, spoken style mixed in with unexpected quotes and other languages. I think I, and John and Frank, were all influenced by Pound's way of referring to all kinds of things all at once. But Pound did it to make some kind of point, whereas I think we did it because we just liked the splash of it, having everything in. That's true for me, anyway—I liked having the whole world in my poems. Strangely enough, one can get that from Pound and from Eliot.

DK: The way you're talking about Pound reminds me of *The Pisan Cantos,* in which Pound brings in the voices of black soldiers, like in "Canto LXXX": "Ain' committed no federal crime, jes a slaight misdemeanor." I wonder if that kind of incorporation of dialect—a practice which Pound shared with Williams—possibly made Pound especially interesting to the avant-garde poets living in New York during the '60s.

KK: Even take a line in *The Cantos* like "Nancy, where art thou?" Or "white-chested martin, goddamnit!" Even if Pound's context is to say that civilization stinks, there's all this fun, lively language in it. As Frank said, "If you're not writing about the tremendous excitement and richness of life, you may as well not be doing it." Like O'Hara's poem "Second Avenue," whatever it's saying, it's full of everything in the world. That's what is so great about it, so exciting about it.

DK: I wanted to ask you about the New School readings that you organized in the early to mid-1960s. Did you have an overall vision for them?

KK: I just tried to get the best poets I could, and the variety I wanted. I had Auden, and Marianne Moore, and then some of my guys. I wanted to mix them up. I just remembered I had Robert Lowell read as well. I think that the Poetry Project at a certain point opened its gates to more people than I thought they would. They had a reading with Lowell and Ginsberg—why not?

DK: A number of the poets associated with the "Second Generation" of the New York School are known for their rough edges. In many of Berrigan's poems, for instance, we're privy to his really unhealthy habits—his many cans of Pepsis, his prodigious speed consumption, his milk shakes and hamburgers. This is opposed to the haute-cuisine feel of an Ashbery or Schuyler poem—I'm thinking of lines of Schuyler's poems which refer to paté maison and the Concord grape season. At the same time, Berrigan maintains the sense of lightness and sophistication that is often associated with the New York School aesthetic.

KK: Well, John and Frank and I went to Harvard. We were all put on the assembly line to be proper fellows, and to get a good, solid, classical education and to be responsible citizens. Most of the downtown poets weren't on that track. That's another thing about their being younger than we were—we had something to react against that was very strong and very total. What was going on in the literary magazines was absolutely awful, there weren't any good magazines around. But schools of poetry hardly matter—it's friendship and individual talent.

DK: Since you mentioned friendship, I'd like to talk about your collaborations. I'm interested in collaboration especially in relation to the early years of The Poetry Project and the special issue of *Locus Solus*, made up entirely of collaborations, which you edited. Everyone there seemed to be very much involved with ideas of anonymity, appropriation, and collaboration. In many collaborations from that time, the author is at best a shadowy figure. The question "who wrote what line" was often treated as a kind of game.

KK: Ah! There's a question I can answer. I was very interested in collaborations because I had done a lot of collaborations with John Ashbery. We did a series of sestinas called "The Bestiary." We did a whole lot of poems in Paris and in Rome. We'd sit around in a lot of nice places like the garden of the Rodin Museum in Paris and write these poems with crazy rules. For example, there has to be something contrary to fact in every line, as well as the word *silver* and a small animal. I found the act of collaboration inspiring. It was something the French taught me—Breton, Eluard. There's a quote at the beginning of that issue of *Locus Solus*—Harry Mathews found it—from Lautréamont: "La poésie doit être faite par tous. Non par un. Pauvre Hugo! Pauvre Racine! Pauvre Coppée! Pauvre Corneille! Pauvre Boileau! Pauvre Scarron! Tics, tics, et tics." [*"Poetry must be made by everybody. Not by one. Poor Hugo! Poor Racine! (etc.)"*]

DK: Do you think you were doing anything subversive by putting out this issue?

KK: Well, I felt that the teaching and this editing and all the writing I did were for the same interesting cause. Poetry should be exciting and interesting and beautiful and surprising—yes, I was uncomfortable with what poets were seen to be supposed to do. Collaboration was certainly carried on at St. Mark's. I performed there with Allen Ginsberg, and we improvised sestinas, haiku, rhymed couplets, all kinds of things. That was an event which could only be possible at St. Mark's.

DK: Tell me about the readings at the 5 Spot. You read the telephone book to music?

KK: Yes, just a little bit of it. Not the night Billie Holiday sang between my sets. That was another night. But John Ashbery never read there. And Frank disdained it—he may have read once, I don't remember. I was the one who had the most enthusiasm for the jazz-poetry nights. I read about three times. One night I read, and Larry was sitting with some painters, among them Mark Rothko. I read my poems, and Larry said, "What do you think?" Rothko replied, "Why don't these poets make any sense?" The last night I read there, Billie Holiday came. Billie was there at the bar. Mal introduced me to her, and she said to me, "Man, your stuff is just crazy!" I believed—or hoped—that meant "good." That night the audience prevailed upon Billie to sing—it was the night Frank O'Hara would write about in his poem "The Day Lady Died." She almost had no voice—it was like a great old wine that almost tastes like water. Then I got up and read again. The evening ended, except for Frank's poem.

> …and I am sweating a lot by now and thinking of
> leaning on the john door in the 5 Spot
> while she whispered a song along the keyboard
> to Mal Waldron and everyone and I stopped breathing.

What a gift for the immediate! Frank could write fast—he could sit down in the middle of a party and write a poem, and if you went over and talked to him he'd put what you just said into the poem. Amazing. I tried to do that, but I had no success at all.

Ann Lauterbach

...he waiting

...lly's spirit (too close

...nd a hint of mercy in the we...

the wand of the keeper

(circus in town, hand of a stranger)

weighted tents open to all.

Nothing is optional. Nor...

*a*nn lauterbach

was born in 1942 and raised in New York City. By the time she was a teenager, she was already devoted to the visual arts and to writing, and attended the High School of Music and Art as a painting major. She received her B.A. from the University of Wisconsin and attended graduate school at Columbia, where she studied contemporary literature. Lauterbach then moved to London in 1967, where she worked as an editor for Thames & Hudson, as a teacher at Saint Martin's School of Art, and as Director of the Literature Program at the Institute for Contemporary Arts. Returning to New York in 1974, she worked as a consultant for various art galleries including Rosa Esman Gallery and Max Protech Gallery, and was Assistant Director of The Washburn Gallery. She then shifted to teaching, and in 1998 became David & Ruth Schwab III Professor of Language and Literature at Bard College.

Lauterbach's poetry combines a consciousness of process and representation with a very grounded relationship to memory and place. Her poems are at once abstract and lush, and have always reminded me of baroque if nonrepresentational brush strokes. Reading Lauterbach in the context of her commitment to visual arts is extremely helpful; she has written poems inspired by the artist Joseph Cornell, for example, and has collaborated with the artist Joe Brainard. Lauterbach has also written about and collaborated with John Ashbery a great deal, so I'd recommend reading Ashbery and Lauterbach in unison. You might detect similar aesthetic concerns, including a deep love for the surface textures of language and an interest in the fragment as a unit of composition. If you can get your hands on it, you should listen to the recording of Lauterbach and Ashbery reading Ashbery's poem "Litany" out loud. "Litany" is a poem written in two voices, represented by two separate columns of text, designed to be read simultaneously! This will give you an idea of Lauterbach's interest in play, as well as her freedom from narrative discourse.

Lauterbach has published numerous collections of poetry including *If in Time: Selected Poems 1975–2002* (Penguin, 2001); *On a Stair* (Penguin, 1997); *And for Example* (Penguin, 1994); and *Clamor* (Penguin, 1992). If you're new to Lauterbach's work, I would recommend reading *If in Time,* which gathers work from several books, but differs from many selected poems in that the order of the poems is reverse-chronological, allowing readers the opportunity to go backwards in time through her writing life. Discover how Lauterbach has moved from a relatively conventional poetics of observation to the far more abstract mode that she writes in today.

[On (Open)]

Sheaf or sheet or sheer (hearing
a turn closer than
an island, proportion of mind
as a circle (sorrow comes round
voracious and pungent
girl meets boy the waiting emblem
geography's spirit (too close to count)
and a hint of mercy in the weeds, the goodly weeds,
the wand of the keeper
(circus in town, hand of a stranger)
weighted tents open to all.
Nothing is optional. Nothing closed.

Daniel Kane: Your poem "On (Open)" reminds me a lot of George Herbert's "Prayer," which is composed of a series of apparently disconnected phrases that, by the end of the poem, read as a connected series of praise—the "prayer" of the poem. Do you see your poem as a "whole," a text that is in service of an overall aesthetic, philosophical, or even moral gesture? Or is your poem a series of fragments?

Ann Lauterbach: I don't want, and I don't think it is necessary, to choose between fragments and wholes. I know this is confusing, but I have come to believe in the notion of whole fragments: pieces of experience, or language, which are understandable and complete in themselves, but which don't necessarily link up with or to a Big Truth or Story or Conclusion. I think our real lives are made up of just such discontinuous fragments—a cup of coffee, the sight of a cardinal in a tree, a kiss, a poem, a scrap of overheard conversation, an image from an ad on TV, an article about Rwanda. The list is endless, and most of these are neither memorable nor important in the "scheme of things," but taken together they make up our daily lives.

I think we need to be glad for these bits and pieces, and not insist that they have to fit into some big picture, some imposed coherence. If you extend the notion from one's own personal life to the life of the planet, of the universe, you see how the notion of consistency and wholeness begins to waver; you see that the model is one taken from scientific paradigms in which everything fits. But many things don't "fit," and as long as we insist on the neatness of the fit, many things of potential significance will be left out, omitted, forgotten. Fragments in this sense suggest the possibility of variety and difference rather than coherence and sameness. They make us think again about what is considered important, or beautiful, or true (you can put any value in here), and so perhaps give us permission to resist moral or aesthetic absolutes. Reality is an invention, a selection, an artifice, not something that actually exits out there/in here in toto.

"On (Open)" is one of several poems in the book *On a Stair* with the title "On," followed by a modifier—"thing," "open," "word," and so forth. These short poems were written to give the book a kind of punctuation or pause, since the poems in the book are so diverse in form; and many are long and divided into several internal parts. So the "On" poems were there to give the reader a breather between the larger discontinuities of the book, as a kind of motif.

I like prepositions a lot (as did Gertrude Stein and William Carlos Willliams) because they signify relation: how one thing is in relation to another, which is how we build up our pictures of the world. They are the places of synapse, or joint, in the scaffold or skeleton of English. They are really nice fragments of language.

DK: "On (Open)" reveals the figure of the clown / magician / circus that is echoed throughout your book *On a Stair.* You write:

> the wand of the keeper
> (circus in town, hand of a stranger)
> weighted tents open to all.

Are you suggesting that poetry itself is magic, since writing is in a kind of artifice—invention, pulling rabbits out of thin air, so to speak?

AL: Well, yes. I think I make an alliance between poets and magicians and nomads: persons who have no fixed place in the scheme of things but who live on the outskirts or the periphery. I think this is a nice place to be, even if it is precarious and scary. The line "(circus in town, hand of a stranger)" is in fact a reference to an early childhood experience, when I was walking through the crowds of a circus and I was holding the hand of someone I thought was my mother, but when I looked up it turned out to be a complete stranger. I was terrified. But I also think it gave me a beginning trust in something outside my own control or knowledge; I was exhilarated by the sense of mystery and danger at the same time as I was frightened. (The stranger helped me locate my mother.) At that moment the world seemed to open up into myriad possibilities—some awful, some wonderful—and it is probably good that it was at a circus where there was already so much fantasy and otherness present. The allure of the unknown is central to all creative practice as far as I can figure out.

Beyond that, there is no doubt that when I was quite young I thought words were magic, quite literally, that they had some kind of power to make things happen, to make people do things or be things. I recall thinking that the dictionary was the place where all power—in the sense of magic as well as the answer to all the questions—resided.

The poem strikes me now as having a sexual or gender aspect. Those opening words ("sheaf/sheet/sheer") all contain the word *she*. The word *hearing,* which follows, alerts the reader to listen to the words rather than just notice them as things. And the whole notion of "open" is complicated from a woman's view: There is a subtext in the book that involves aspects of trust/fidelity/closure as opposed to openness/promiscuity/possibility. It's a curious and strange dichotomy that doesn't break apart along conventional lines of good/bad.

DK: The last phrase in your poem ("Nothing closed") bears a certain affinity to Robert Duncan's "opening of the field," or even John Ashbery's "What Is Poetry," which ends with the question: "It might give us—what?—some flowers soon?" I mention these other poems to suggest that "On (Open)" is part of a tradition of anti-closure, one in which the poem encourages or even demands multiple interpretations as opposed to more "right answers." Do you agree with this reading? If so, what is the reader supposed to do if nothing is closed?

AL: The thing that is confusing about this last line is the odd pairing of "optional" with "closed." If nothing is optional, it means you have to choose, or even that the choices are determined; either way, the choices you make will have consequences in your life and in the lives of others, so it isn't just "anything goes." Freedom is about the nature of limits; without limits, freedom is meaningless. So one's sense of moving through the world is, in a sense, conditioned, on the one hand, by how important it is to understand what you are doing or being, to be conscious, and, on the other, by the need to have a belief or trust in the open bearing of the world.

As far as interpretations are concerned, I think that there are many possible, right interpretations of a given poem, but I think there are more wrong ones. The thing I am not interested in is having a reader align her or his thoughts about a poem with my own. The reader has experiences, intuitions, which are different from mine, and I am not particularly interested in her—in your—identifying with me per se. The reader does not have to know about the experience I described above about the circus in order to "get" something from that line; if she or he does, I have failed as a poet. But I don't want a sort of free association either—I think that language binds us to meanings. But the content, or subject matter, is open. Your questions all point to a certain set of thoughts about this poem and others, and that set is right, as far as I am concerned, because you bring to the poem your habit of reading and your interest in words.

DK: One of the things I've noticed in this poem and in other poems in *On a Stair* is your surprising use of seemingly archaic turns of phrase and language. Here, the phrase "the goodly weeds" suggests Old or Renaissance-style English. It also suggests a ballad, as in "The Ballad of the Goodly Weeds." Was this a self-conscious move on your part, and if so, what might a student of poetry get out of using "old-fashioned" language in a post-modern poem?

AL: I am hardly the only poet to do this sort of thing. It is a sign, I guess, of a pleasure in the flavors and distinctions of English diction. The "weeds," you know, they were what widows wore as well as the unwanted plants (some of which are very beautiful) in a garden. I suppose the widow and the weeds are part of the same space of outcast or uncared-for characters/objects that are included in the nexus of the clown.

I don't write with strategies. I trust something about language to "pull" things toward the poem which the poem needs or wants. *Goodly* is not a word we hear much, but it brings me into a sort of *ur*-place which I think is related to Puritan New England, where one part of my heritage is. I think the important word here is *mercy*, which gives the poem an overall "religious" feeling. I love the histories of words, their etymologies. Emerson says "every word was once a fossil poem," and he is right. If you look up the word *mercy* you find an amazing array: it is related to the French word for "thank you," of course, *merci*. In my dictionary, under the synonyms, there is this list: "clemency, lenity, charity, grace: mercy, a word of much emotional force and hence one applicable to extreme situations, indicates a kindly refraining from inflicting punishment or pain, often a refraining brought about by genuinely felt compassion or sympathy, or a general disposition towards these latter characteristics. ('Earthly power doth then show likest God's when mercy seasons justice.')" Not to be pious, but I think we as a society could do with a whole lot more mercy.

DK: "*Girl meets boy* the waiting emblem" is a very rich line for me. Again, I'm brought back in time, to medieval emblem books, Books of Hours, psalters. In these kinds of texts, one might see an image of a couple that is laden with allusive potential—girl and boy as Adam and Eve, for example. How are you using the girl and boy in this poem?

AL: I seem to be attracted to words like *emblem* and *insignia*. Things that are signs of/for things—as words, of course, are. This central construction of Eros, of the animating potential of Love, is for me at the core of a lot of what I write—that, and its opposites, loss and solitude. I think of Love not necessarily in its romantic—and at this point debased—form (although that too!), but as an emblem of everything that makes us feel able to do what we need and want to do. I think of Eros as a crucial, powerful, central animating human force—sometimes, as we know, a very destructive one when it is blind and blindly intolerant. I'm less interested in how this force has been domesticated and trivialized. I guess I am drawn to a very early, even pre-Christian, idea of a generative (creative/destructive) spirit.

I want to imagine a world in which faith, belief, trust, desire, hope, mercy, and love are attached to secular places, or are at least not constrained or contained in a given religion's laws or customs. It isn't about a higher authority. But it is about a certain kind of humility and wonder.

DK: Since this interview is in part intended for students, could you say something about using fragments in poetry?

AL: There are only fragments. The world is far bigger and more complex than any picture or whole we mere mortals can come up with. Language is a nice structure into which to place your fragments. If you learn its complexities, vagaries, subtleties—how malleable it is—if you understand language as a sort of fluid whole, a multifarious thing, then your fragments will be fine. You can make wholes from them if you need to, or you can leave them as fragments, as long as you care for (pay attention to) the language itself: how it "works."

DK: Is there a method or series of steps that you might recommend teachers to take in presenting "On (Open)" to high school students not so familiar with poetry?

AL: A poem is not a puzzle to be solved. A poem is an experience, an event, in and of language. It should be approached as such:

- What kind of event happened to you when you read this poem?
- Did you get a feeling?
- Did you have an idea?
- Did you get reminded of something?
- Did you go elsewhere, away from the familiar world into another, stranger, one?
- Did you look up words and find out new meanings, as you would ask directions in a strange city?
- Why do you think the poet made this word choice, and not another?
- Why do you think the line is broken here, at this word, and not at another?
- How is a line break in a poem different from a comma or a period in a prose sentence?

As long as teachers think poems have to be translated, students will be fearful that they don't have access to the "right" language. The logic of poetry is not the same as the logic of a story or a newspaper article. Poetry is often as much about the way language works—rhythms and sounds and syntax, musical rather than pictorial values—as it is "about" a given subject. The meanings which come to a poem are often just at the intersection between these elements. Students of poetry should become excited about the fact of language as such. Some poems are more difficult than others, the fact of language as such. Some poems are more difficult than others, but then, some experiences are too. It isn't the worst thing in the world to be confused, if the confusion is honest—that is, I don't set out to write poems that are difficult or confusing. I like to provoke; I want my poems to give people permission to think for themselves, on the one hand, and to be deeply responsive, on the other.

Bernadette Mayer

Nowadays you guys settle for
By a soporific color cable t.v.
Instead of any arc of love, no
The G.I. Joe team blows it ev

Wake up! It's the middle of t
You can either make love or

the Col

To make love, turn to page 12

bernadette mayer

was born in Brooklyn in 1945. After the death of her father in 1958 and of her mother in 1960, Mayer basically raised herself and her sister Rosemary. She became a student at the New School for Social Research in New York City and received her B.A. in 1967. At the New School, she met and was influenced by poets associated with the New York School, including Bill Berkson and Kenneth Koch. In the social milieu of the 1960s poetry renaissance on the Lower East Side of Manhattan, Mayer befriended poets Ron Padgett, Anne Waldman, Lewis Warsh, Alice Notley, Clark Coolidge, Ted Berrigan, and others. From 1972 to 1974, she edited and published the influential journal *0 to 9* with the conceptual artist and writer Vito Acconci, and with her partner Lewis Warsh, Mayer ran United Artists Press. UAP published the work of many of the writers associated with the American avant-garde poetry scene, including Robert Creeley, James Schuyler, Notley, Padgett, Berrigan, Berkson, Waldman, and others. In the 1980s, Mayer served as the director of The Poetry Project in New York City, where she has also taught writing workshops. She currently lives and works in upstate New York in a big converted church in the Berkshires.

To get a sense of where Mayer is coming from as a poet, you would do well to start by checking out her theoretical ideas regarding the practice of poetry, which have had an significant influence on the teaching of writing. Read through Mayer's legendary and widely-circulated "experiments list" (available online at www.poetryproject.org). The list is composed of an ever-evolving set of writing exercises, including: "Systematically eliminate the use of certain kinds of words or phrases from a piece of writing: eliminate all adjectives from a poem of your own, or take out all words beginning with *s* in Shakespeare's sonnets," and "Rewrite someone else's writing. Experiment with theft and plagiarism." Such exercises point to Mayer's radical if whimsical challenge to formalist convention and authorial stability and privilege, a challenge that is consistently manifested in Mayer's various writings.

Mayer is a poet who has steadfastly tracked and transcribed consciousness, using dreams, psychology, letters, epigrams, and science writing at various intervals. Her focus on collage techniques, stream-of-consciousness writing, and chance-operation poems has established her as one of the most innovative poets around. Such writing practices reveal Mayer's various influences: the work of Gertrude Stein and James Joyce, the Dadaists, and the chance-determined compositions of John Cage. Mayer has also been credited with influencing the New York wing of the Language school—among them, Charles Bernstein, Peter Seaton, and Nick Piombino, all of whom participated in Mayer's workshops.

Mayer is the author of numerous books, including: *Two Haloed Mourners: Poems* (Granary Books, 1998), *The Desires of Mothers to Please Others in Letters* (Hard Press, 1994), *Sonnets* (Tender Buttons, 1989), and *Midwinter Day* (Turtle Island, 1982). I would recommend beginning with *A Bernadette Mayer Reader* (New Directions, 1992)—a great, if too slim, volume of Mayer's selected work, which opens with her earliest stuff from the 1960s and progresses right through the end of the '80s. I was hooked on her work from the start, and I am now the proud owner of nearly everything she's written!

[Sonnet]

There was a man on 8th Street
        around independence day
Looking for help to get back to his house
The old man said, Now you're going to see
        something you've never seem before
We guided him there behind the locked door
        up the indoor stairs to the outdoor floor
            and there were flowers and 7 doors
                he was ninety-four
On 13th street a stoop and the front
        of a tenement collapsed
For no reason killing Evelyn
        who was in Sophia's class
Right around independence day an american
        something
Shot down an Iranian passenger plane saying
        it was an accident or tragedy
Killing everybody nobody's ever gonna know
        what really happened
Some people die you know them right next door
Other ones they die what seems like anonymously
        in a war
Some do both things or all three and now
You are going to see something you've never seen before
Up the indoor stairs behind the locked door
        we guided him there

* He said the landlord paid him two months rent to move
in forty years ago and there were no other tenants for
a year

Daniel Kane: Why are you attracted to the sonnet form?

Bernadette Mayer: I like the sonnet form because it gives you the chance to develop some thought, and then come to a conclusion. It's all totally false—that's not how you really think, but in a way, it is how you think. So that's why sonnets are interesting. Sonnets pretend to reflect the way you think. That's always been my theory.

DK: You mean when you have a thought, your mind runs through it, and then your eyebrows dart up in a kind of pleasurable acknowledgment that there is now a sense of conclusion?

BM: Yes. It's weird, because it's not the way you'd want people to respond at a poetry reading. You wouldn't want them to say, "Aha!"

DK: Does the way you use the sonnet, especially in the poem, "Sonnet," fight against the form? What I love about this poem is that there's a sense of mystery throughout the whole thing. Were you consciously playing with the expectation of a reader who, this being called a "sonnet," would assume his or her eyebrows were probably going to go up in the end?

BM: Yes. My poem has a footnote at the end, but you can't figure out where that note belongs. I'm talking about those final two lines, which break the fourteen-line "rule":

> He said the landlord paid him two months rent to move
> in forty years ago and there were no other tenants for
> a year

DK: I love the footnote. How would you explain that footnote to the reader who might protest, "Hey, what's that doing there?!"

BM: After writing the poem, I wanted to explain what the old man had said to us about the landlord. It would also be interesting to tell kids about the numbers in the poem. I noticed that there are a lot of numbers in this poem, so then I started mentioning as many numbers as I could. I figured, "It's a number poem!" Also, of course, a sonnet is famous for having a certain number of lines, even though it doesn't really. Fourteen lines is the traditional kind of sonnet, but a sonnet until recently could be as long as fifteen, sixteen, seventeen, or eighteen lines. When I say "recently," I'm talking about the sixteenth century.

DK: Footnote business aside, I thought it was funny the way you snuck around that fourteen-line rule by indenting the lines. It's still fourteen lines.

BM: Right, the lines are so long, and that's why I decided to indent them, to stick with the fourteen-line rule. But there is that addendum, so the poem is really just a hoax. But as long as it looks good I think it's okay! [*laughs*]

DK: Now what would a kid learn about sonnets from reading "Sonnet," assuming the kid was determined to consider a poem a sonnet if it followed the Petrarchan or Shakespearean templates?

BM: I think it's important to tell children—or anyone who's learning about poetry—that a sonnet isn't always a fourteen-line poem. Many ancient authors wrote sonnets that were longer or shorter than what many of us might imagine a sonnet should be. Catullus wrote eleven-line poems that were twelve lines long. I think if you tell somebody a form is a certain length, they really believe you, and that's too bad. Catullus didn't write sonnets, of course. He wrote in hendecasyllables, which are eleven-syllable lines, and then a lot of them were twelve-syllable lines. In other languages or in other times, people broke these rules all the time. I'm sure they took the rules seriously, but they seriously broke them. That's kind of fun, actually, breaking the rules. It also calls attention to the way in which you broke the rules.

DK: In a weird sort of way, breaking these rules manages to confirm the strength of the "conservative" Petrarchan or Shakespearean sonnet, because our attention is drawn to how the sonnet is supposed to be—we contrast the new rule-breaking sonnet with the law-abiding one. What about other formal decisions you made? I'm thinking about rhyme: a lot of students' rhyming poetry tends to alternate between a rap-style bravado and a Hallmark-style sentimentality. How would you teach this poem as a model for surprising and fresh uses of rhyme?

BM: I always thought that rhymes were interesting if the words looked the same and if they were directly underneath each other. That's what happens in this poem. If you're talking about the *doors*, *four*, *before*, *floor*, I must say that was all an accident. It just worked out that way.

DK: So your rhymes weren't entirely intentional—that's interesting. I noticed that you've placed the words *collapsed* and *class* so that they work as a slant rhyme, which I really like. Slant rhymes can be a healthy alternative for young writers to consider. Do you ever read students' rhyming poetry and want to run away, locking the door behind you?

BM: Well, I made my students at the Staten Island school I've taught at join the Rhymers Anonymous group.

DK: Were there a lot of members?

BM: Oh, yes. They loved it. Twelve-step programs for rhymers proved very popular. Before they joined the program, I asked them what their favorite poem was, and they'd respond with that Valentine's Day poem, "Roses are red, violets are blue." After all, it rhymes! And then they would rhyme every poem. One woman in the same class made much more money than I ever did as a poet by selling a poem she had written to a greeting card company. It rhymed—boy, did it rhyme!

DK: In Rhymers Anonymous, was the purpose to wean students off of rhyme?

BM: Yes, definitely.

DK: But you use rhymes—fairly traditional ones, at that.

BM: Sure, well, that's breaking my own rules, which I encourage! [*laughs*]

DK: At moments like this, I think of Whitman's "Do I contradict myself? / Very well then I contradict myself, / (I am large, I contain multitudes.)" But perhaps to rhyme imaginatively, one initially has to take a break from rhyming, think about how one tends to rhyme in predictable, familiar ways, and then finally start rhyming in an interesting way.

BM: Hopefully you can do both things—rhyme, not rhyme. If you want to break bad rhyming habits, using internal rhymes is fun.

DK: Can we talk a little bit about the role of mystery in "Sonnet"? I'm thinking in particular of the final couplet:

> You are going to see something you've never seen before
> Up the indoor stairs behind the locked door
>   we guided him there

BM: There's no mystery about it to me. Does it seem mysterious to you?

DK: It does, because the hint of "something you've never seen before" sets me up for an answer or revelation at the end of the poem. But it's a ruse; the final line ("we guided him there") doesn't even have a period to indicate closure! It ends on an open note. The monster I expected to see in the living room or the old guy's dead mother sitting in a rocking chair— they aren't in the poem.

BM: In reality, though, the guy just meant that he was paid to live in this place, which I had never seen before. That's all he meant. That's the job of the addendum, to clear that up. This guy's apartment was off West 8th Street, near all those shoe stores.

DK: Can you tell us more about the names and places in this poem?

BM: Sure. Sophia is my daughter, and Evelyn was her friend at school. Evelyn was sitting on her stoop and it collapsed underneath her.

DK: You mention these personal events, and you also allude to political events, like the time when an American warplane shot down an Iranian passenger plane. However, you don't sound like you're unfurling banners or putting on your combat boots. How would you suggest that young writers integrate their political opinions into their poetry?

BM: That's a difficult question. I wrote a Utopia, a whole book in which I got political. A lot of people have said it's my worst book, but a lot of people say it's my best book, so who knows? I don't think I can be directly political, but some people can be. Allen Ginsberg was good at political writing. Catullus wrote great poems making fun of Julius Caesar. Paul Goodman also wrote great political poems. I don't know if you can still get Goodman's *Collected Poems*, but read it if you can.

DK: Is there such a thing as a popular poet for students who might not be in the "poetry world"?

BM: I once asked some of my students, who were college age, who their favorite American poet was, and they said Jim Morrison. I had made a bet with them that whoever it was, I'd teach that poet for a week, so I had to teach Jim Morrison for a week. I actually grew to like him! You know who's a good poet? Leonard Cohen—he's popular, I guess. Patti Smith is an interesting writer, too.

DK: People could teach Patti Smith as an introduction to a lesson on Rimbaud, maybe?

BM: That would be fun. I made my students write down the words to the Led Zeppelin song "Stairway to Heaven," because they kept mentioning it, and actually it's a pretty good poem.

DK: Really? Even with "There's a lady who knows / all that glitters is gold"?

BM: Well, that doesn't sound very good, does it? [*laughs*]

DK: Let's get back to the sonnet form. What if William Shakespeare were to walk up to you one day and ask you, "Bernadette, how does your poem fit into the definition of the word *sonnet*?" How would you respond?

BM: First, I'd invite him to dinner. He'd be a good guest. We could eat rabbit, stuff like that. And then I'd say, "William, it has fourteen lines!" And then he'd probably say, in a dubious tone, "Yeah, fourteen lines." Then we'd see what happens next.

DK: Is there anything else you'd want to say to me about this poem? Imagine I'm thirteen, and I'm looking out the classroom window, maybe not paying attention.

BM: I would just say write any way you want. You can make the lines short or long. And looking out the window is a good way to write a poem. A good way to write a sonnet is to walk fourteen blocks. Write one line for each block. I know a poet, Bill Kushner, who used to do that. I used to see him all the time with his notebook on the street. You can do it easily in a city, because there are so many words all around.

Harryette Mullen

...t the bargains tha...
Walt's sheep. Yet
platonic honoure...
My Mickey Mous...
d Yet, by hal...

harryette mullen

was born in Florence, Alabama, and raised in Fort Worth, Texas. A city with a rich musical tradition, Fort Worth was home to W. C. Handy, self-proclaimed "father of the blues"; Townes Van Zandt; Willie "Prince" Lasha (whose daughters lived across the street from the Mullens); and noted free-jazz innovator Ornette Coleman. (Coleman's music, like Mullen's poetry, often suggests or quotes from childhood nursery songs and playground rhymes.) Mullen's love of words was instilled at a very early age by reading family copies of the Bible, an unabridged *Webster's Dictionary*, *Roget's Thesaurus*, *Complete Works of Shakespeare*, and the *World Book Encyclopedia*. One of her favorite memories is sitting on her grandfather's lap while he read nursery rhymes from a large illustrated *Mother Goose*. "In some mysterious way," Mullen says, "all of this has something to do with my growing up to be a poet." She has worn many hats: waiting tables in a bar, typing itemized bills in a law office, working as a receptionist at Goodwill, taking orders at a Jack-in-the-Box, sweeping the floor of a florist shop, and assisting a grouchy caterer. Most of Mullen's professional career, however, has been in the field of teaching and writing. Mullen received a B.A. in English from the University of Texas and a Ph.D. from the University of California, Santa Cruz. She is currently a professor of English and African American Studies at the University of California, Los Angeles.

Mullen's poetry, like that of many of the poets in this book, draws upon "popular" culture—pop music, cartoons, and children's games. In Mullen's case, the earliest poems and lyrics that influenced her were *Mother Goose*, jump rope rhymes, and playing "the dozens." Mullen's childhood was also enlivened by church hymns, R&B and pop songs on the radio, Gilbert and Sullivan operettas, folk songs, Gershwin's *Porgy and Bess*, and jazz divas Sarah Vaughan and Nancy Wilson. One can find echoes, allusions, and quotations of these sources—along with church, folk and blues music by Odetta, Leadbelly, Pete Seeger, and music anthologized on the

Alan Lomax folklore recordings—throughout Mullen's work. Mullen also recalls the importance of memorizing Langston Hughes's "Mother to Son" and James Weldon Johnson's "The Creation."

Mullen's volumes of poetry include *Sleeping with the Dictionary* (University of California Press, 2002), *Muse & Drudge* (Singing Horse, 1995), *S*PeRM**K*T* (Singing Horse, 1992), and *Trimmings* (Tender Buttons, 1991). The first book I read of Mullen's was *S*PerM**K*T*—the fragmented, hilarious, intellectual, and moving references to contemporary consumer culture were absolutely fascinating to me. *Muse & Drudge* might be a good place to start as well, since the meter is clearly indebted to hip-hop rhythms. To find out about *Sleeping with the Dictionary,* read our interview!

[Dim Lady]

My honeybunch's peepers are nothing like neon. Today's special at Red Lobster is redder than her kisser. If Liquid Paper is white, her racks are institutional beige. If her mop were Slinkys, dishwater Slinkys would grow on her noggin. I have seen tablecloths in Shakey's Pizza Parlors, red and white, but no such picnic colors do I see in her mug. And in some minty-fresh mouthwashes there is more sweetness than in the garlic breeze my main squeeze wheezes. I love to hear her rap, yet I'm aware that Muzak has a hipper beat. I don't know any Marilyn Monroes. My ball and chain is plain from head to toe. And yet, by gosh, my scrumptious Twinkie has as much sex appeal for me as any lanky model or platinum movie idol who's hyped beyond belief.

[Variations on a Theme Park]

My Mickey Mouse ears are nothing like sonar. Colorado is far less rusty than Walt's lyric riddles. If sorrow is wintergreen, well then Walt's breakdancers are dunderheads. If hoecakes are Wonder Bras, blond Wonder Bras grow on Walt's hornytoad. I have seen roadkill damaged, riddled and wintergreen, but no such roadkill see I in Walt's checkbook. And in some purchases there is more deliberation than in the bargains that my Mickey Mouse redeems. I love to herd Walt's sheep, yet well I know that muskrats have a far more platonic sonogram. I grant I never saw a googolplex groan. My Mickey Mouse, when Walt waddles, trips on garbanzos. And yet, by halogen-light, I think my loneliness as reckless as any souvenir bought with free coupons.

Daniel Kane: My college students, who are generally not versed in avant-gardist work, really "got" your book *Muse & Drudge*—maybe due to the fact that it seems influenced by hip-hop, has an abundance of popular and race-specific references, and consistently rhymes! Could you talk about what influenced the book?

Harryette Mullen: As much as I claim Jean Toomer, Langston Hughes, Gwendolyn Brooks, Melvin Tolson, Bob Kaufman, Margaret Walker, and the poets of the Black Arts movement as literary ancestors, Language-oriented poets are important influences on my work, from the paratactic prose poetry of my books *Trimmings* and *S*PeRM**K*T* to my desire, in *Muse & Drudge,* to write a poem that encourages collaborative reading across cultural boundaries. I might add that my connection to the Language poets of the Bay Area was through Nathaniel Mackey and Gloria Watkins, just as my link to poetry of the New York School, Umbra, and Black Arts movement was through Lorenzo Thomas.

  Muse & Drudge, like Toni Morrison's *Jazz* with its multiple narrators, employs not one but a chorus of possible "speakers" or "singers." They include, among others, lyric poet Sappho and blues singer Bessie Smith. Having considered the mnemonic force of jingles in *S*PeRM**K*T,* I also wanted to suggest, with *Muse & Drudge,* that rhyme is too powerful a tool to be abandoned to advertising, greeting cards, or even platinum rap recordings. I hoped to reclaim it. It's interesting that you say *Muse & Drudge* is more accessible. I think that my other books are easier to follow in that they are more coherently organized texts. But the apparently orderly verse form and recurrent tropes of *Muse & Drudge* allow readers to experience it as extended lyric. It has a musical quality that attracted the attention of two composers, T. J. Anderson and Christine Baczewska, who have set parts of *Muse & Drudge.*

DK: How important are considerations of race in your writing?

HM: For me, race, class, and gender have been significant issues, but of course they are not the whole of identity, and certainly they are not the sum of my poetry—or of anyone's poetry, for that matter. I can be a black woman while chewing gum and thinking about Disneyland or supermarkets, while reading Stein or Shakespeare, just as I can be a black woman contemplating conventional representations of black women in literature, media, and popular culture. Living in California, where white people are a minority, I'm not so sure that my identity or experience is "marginal." As a woman and as a person of color, I belong to two global majorities, but I'm also aware that throughout most of history, it is not the majority that rules but a privileged minority.

DK: So does identity inform your poetics as much as what might be considered more traditionally formal concerns?

HM: Whatever the content of the poem, identity (not just my own) is as much an aspect of the work as a concern with language, poetics, and form. I think this is evident in all of my work, whether I was consciously constructing a "black voice" or "black literary style" in my first book, *Tree Tall Woman*; writing "the new sentence" in *Trimmings* and *S*PeRM**K*T*; experimenting with "kinky quatrains" in *Muse & Drudge*; or playing Oulipo word games with my *American Heritage* in my latest book, *Sleeping with the Dictionary*. My focus on the clash of feminism with fashion in *Trimmings* and my take on advertising and consumption in *S*PeRM**K*T* were also informed by my perspective as a black woman, and so was my approach to the politics of language and dialect in *Sleeping with the Dictionary*. We often tend to reduce and simplify black expressive traditions, and we must acknowledge the diversity and hybridity of those traditions. I agree with the critic Margo Jefferson when she says, regarding the creation of jazz, "Race is not just a series of obstacles, but it's also a set of possibilities."

DK: Could you discuss your use of word games and Oulipo-inspired procedures in *Sleeping with the Dictionary*? Are these kinds of language games a way of undermining identity and associating oneself with a kind of cosmopolitanism, as opposed to a regionalist voice?

HM: Well, I thought I was working "beyond category" (as Ellington said of his compositions that mix jazz and classical influences) in my earlier books. A few of the poems in *Sleeping with the Dictionary* are older than *Muse & Drudge*. As language and identity come together in the work, a concern with collective experience and cultural representation may be more evident in some poems, while wordplay and poetic experiment are more conspicuous in others. I don't know if I'm undermining identity so much as continually rewriting and revising it.

What attracts me to the Oulipo writers, besides their sense of humor, is their systematic effort to demystify the poetic process. In their practice, writing is a pleasurable game that may result in works of "potential literature." Their research reveals that devices we associate with the work of avant-garde or experimental writers are also found in ancient texts, and even in oral forms such as riddles and jokes.

DK: Could you name a couple of these games?

HM: Many quatrains in *Muse & Drudge* began with double entendres, puns, and other polysemic wordplay. Sometimes familiar material is transformed by linguistic scrambling or various kinds of cryptographic writing. In *Sleeping with the Dictionary,* I'm playing with anagrams, palindromes, homophones, and other devices favored by Oulipo. (By the way, I've published critical articles about Sandra Cisneros's cryptographic writing in *Woman Hollering Creek* and the brain-teasing puns in *Oreo,* by Fran Ross, if anyone's interested.)

DK: When you talk about Oulipo as demystifying the poetic process, I'm interested in your attention to audience, as "demystifying" suggests greater accessibility. Who was your audience in *Muse & Drudge*?

HM: The audience, as always, is any interested reader. But of all my books since *Tree Tall Woman, Muse & Drudge* has the clearest Afrocentric vision. It was in part a response to extreme representations of black women in the media as welfare queens, drug addicts, and skanky prostitutes on the one hand, or as fabulous divas and fashion supermodels on the other. In retrospect, that onslaught of bipolar media images now seems to have been coordinated with the war on drugs, the growth of the prison industrial system, and attacks on affirmative action, welfare, and proposals for universal health care throughout the 1980s and early '90s. *Trimmings* and

S*PeRM**K*T are in dialogue with the modernism of Gertrude Stein, whose work influenced Richard Wright and was known to writers of the Harlem Renaissance through their mutual friend Carl Van Vechten.

My sources for *Muse & Drudge* were traditional or familiar materials from African American culture, popular culture, and mass media, but in most cases I sampled and altered the material through some kind of textual device. In composing the quatrains, usually I'd improvise on some fragment of "blacklore":

> tom-tom can't catch
> a green cabin
> ginger hebben as
> ancestor dances in Ashanti

Sometimes the improvisations are punning riffs on sound, leaning toward a kind of jazzy scat or hip-hop style:

> divine sunrises
> Osiris's irises
> his splendid mistress
> is his sis Isis

In one quatrain, I borrowed Shakespeare's device of writing his name into his sonnets. Some scholars argue that, in addition to punning on "Will" in his poetry, he's subliminally woven his surname into the sonnet that begins "The expense of spirit." There's also a tradition of poets referring to themselves in ghazals. I took this idea of a poetic signature when I wrote a quatrain using echoes of my own name, Harryette Romell Mullen:

> marry at a hotel, annul 'em
> nary hep male rose sullen
> let alley roam, yell melon
> dull normal fellow hammers omelet

DK: Do you think of *Sleeping with the Dictionary* as a new departure?

HM: As I suppose my title implies, *Sleeping with the Dictionary* explores my ambivalent relation to language, both standard and vernacular dialects of American English. The idea is that the dictionary can be not only an authoritative reference, but also a more intimate companion, so to speak. It is literally true that I sometimes fall asleep with books I've taken to bed, including the big dictionary. It's significant to me that my *American Heritage Dictionary* was compiled with the aid of a usage panel that included African American writers Langston Hughes and Arna Bontemps, as well as feminist author Gloria Steinem. Thanks to my mother, an elementary school teacher, I have loved encyclopedias and dictionaries since childhood. Along with other volumes, my shelf includes *A Feminist Dictionary,* compiled by Paula Treichler and Cheris Kramarae, and Clarence Major's *Juba to Jive: A Dictionary of African American Slang,* an important source for the lexicon of *Muse & Drudge.*

DK: I'm fascinated by the fact that you did things that usually are outside the purview of the author—choosing the cover art of *Muse & Drudge,* for example, or having Henry Louis Gates and Sandra Cisneros "blurb" your book.

HM: The choices I made were part conscious, part intuitive, part serendipitous. A benefit of working with small independent presses is that authors can be more involved in such decisions. In my experience, each cover has been a collaboration of publisher, author, and artist/designer. Even the university presses allowed me to choose the cover art, since I was willing to find the artists and get their permission. All of my publishers have encouraged my active participation, if only because they lack the resources to do everything themselves. Many poetry books don't get reviewed, so often the work falls into an abyss of silence. I want to do what I can to help audiences find my work, including discussing it with readers, critics, teachers, and students as I travel around to various literary events.

DK: You once described to me your idea of an "aesthetic apartheid." Could you expand on that term, especially as it relates to experimental writing and social injustice?

HM: As Erica Hunt reminds us in her lucid essay, "Notes for an Opposi-tional Poetics," aesthetic and political opposition to the status quo do not necessarily go hand in hand, nor are they mutually exclusive. I'm inter-ested in the shared aspirations of social and aesthetic movements that envi-sion a better world. While I celebrate the differences that create distinct aesthetic preferences, I seek to overcome the social segregation that enforces aesthetic apartheid. In Los Angeles, for example, this might require that I drive out of my own familiar neighborhood to see an art exhibit in Little Tokyo or attend a poetry reading at the Institute of Italian Culture—to recall a couple of excursions I've made recently—in between taking visitors to the Watts Towers and to the World Stage in Leimert Park.

DK: This sense of political and social engagement is certainly clear in all your books. When in *Muse & Drudge* you write, "how a border orders disor-der / how the children looked / whose mothers worked / in the maquila-dora." Immigration and sweatshop conditions seem to have something to do with the form of the poem. Does thinking about form in some way affect the way you read social and political events?

HM: Human beings create meaning by ascribing significance to difference, however arbitrary. The first line of the stanza makes two observations. The separation of a border defines an order that must be defended, and also presupposes a disorder that continually threatens order. Traditionally it's argued that the container of form creates a boundary or frame that sepa-rates order from disorder, art from the mundane. Because our lives encompass a great deal of disorder, we value form and convention. Appar-ently we need boundaries, even imaginary or arbitrary ones, to define social organization and artistic form. Still, it's impossible to regulate absolutely the movement of people across borders, or even to define with certainty the difference between a work of art and a piece of garbage. It's also true that certain artists are regarded as threats to social or political order.

DK: I suddenly had this vision of your work as proposing a new kind of order. In *Muse & Drudge,* for example, you write, "torn veins stitched / together with pine needles / mended hands fix / the memory of a people."

These lines suggest that one is putting history back together again via the juxtaposition of fragments, which suggest a modernist project in many ways. Do you see your work as blurring the boundaries between the modern and the postmodern?

HM: "Putting history back together again" sounds good, and mending ourselves as well. Of course the fragments, however they are arranged, don't add up to a master narrative. I'm aware that some critics see postmodernism as only a later development of the modernist project. Others would say that modernists mourn a shattered world, while postmodernists revel in its fragmentation and lack of coherence. I suppose my own feeling is somewhere between mourning and reveling. There's no time in the past I'd rather live than now, and I can only hope that we all have room for improvement in the future.

DK: It seems to me that *Sleeping with the Dictionary* might especially appeal to students due to its inclusive use of language games. Might you suggest ways in teaching a specific poem from the book to students?

HM: Pronouns are powerful words. Consider how we use "I" and "you," "we" and "they" to divide or unite ourselves. Sometimes when I'm writing, I'll delete the words "I" or "they" and substitute "we" in a poem. It gives the work a different perspective, makes it more inclusive. One of my students wrote a fine essay on how the use of pronouns includes the reader in the poetry of Adrienne Rich and John Ashbery.

I believe my poetry ideas can be adapted to any educational level, in creative writing as well as in literature classes. I often write poems using the same assignments I give my students. "Dim Lady" and "Variation on a Theme Park" came out of an exercise asking students to write parodies of famous sonnets. With different groups I've used sonnets by Shakespeare or Neruda as models, suggesting that students choose a particular rule for transforming the poem. Instead of having students write a précis or paraphrase in prose, teachers could suggest that students rewrite the poem by plugging other words into the same syntactical and rhetorical structure. Students can use the Oulipo N + 7 rule of substituting for each noun in the poem the seventh noun up or down from it in the dictionary.

"Variation on a Theme Park" is a "freestyle" version of this Oulipo game. I didn't count up or down, but for each noun and verb in the original text I substituted a different word that begins with the same letter, using free association and the dictionary for inspiration. Students might substitute synonyms or antonyms to alter the diction of a poem, the way I've used synonymous slang words and commercial brand names in "Dim Lady." They could write "inverse translations" of Neruda sonnets, substituting an antonym for each noun and verb in the poem. They could rewrite a familiar poem or story using periphrasis, as I've done in "European Folk Tale Variant." Here my inspiration was Toni Cade Bambara's hilarious black vernacular revision of "Goldilocks and the Three Bears."

The idea of using inversion or antonyms in a poetic way came from Richard Wilbur's delightful collections of poetry for children. I've used *Runaway Opposites*, with collages by Henrik Drescher, in my university classes. Wilbur's humorous couplets highlight his clever use of rhyme and his unconventional sense of opposition:

> I wonder if you've ever seen a
> willow sheltering a hyena?
> Nowhere in nature can be found
> an opposition more profound:
> A sad tree weeping inconsolably!
> A wild beast laughing uncontrollably!

Who else has ever paired as "opposites" a weeping willow and a laughing hyena? One of my poems in *Sleeping with the Dictionary*, "Way Opposite," is an emulation of Wilbur. Another, "Any Lit," uses as its model a fragment of a traditional African American courtship ritual: "You are a huckleberry beyond my persimmon." My poem was created by substitution, playing on the sounds of "you" and "my" in every line.

Many students have tried acrostic poems. Sometimes in my workshops I give everyone a handful of uncooked alphabet noodles to play with. Scrabble tiles are good, too. The students spell out their own names, then use the letters of their names to write anagrams and acrostics. My poem "Ask Aden" is an acrostic I wrote for my nephew Aden when he was about six years old. That's an age when children ask wonderful, often unanswerable, questions, so I decided that each line of the poem would be a question. Originally this was a small handmade book that was inspired by a set of alphabet stamps. On each rubber stamp the letter was a different animal: an *aardvark* shaped like an *A*, a dragon for *D*, and so on. The word *aardvark* sounds like it contains the word *are*, so the first line of the poem was "Are aardvarks anxious?" That became the model for the other lines. From childhood on, I've associated poetry with games and puzzles, with singing and dancing, with codes and ciphers, with riddles and rhymes. I've never lost that sense of play and pleasure in making poetry.

Michael Palmer

...look at them for...

...ked, and tell me what y...

...cannot I replied
for my eyes have grown su...
from reading too long by c...

Tell me what you've read
said the round and sad-ey...
I cannot I replied

...my memory has gro...
...oking at things...
...f light

michael palmer

was born in 1943 into a middle-class Italian-American family in New York City. He received his B.A. and M.A. from Harvard University, writing his undergraduate thesis on the French poet Raymond Roussel (a proto-surrealist who had an immense influence on John Ashbery). While at Harvard, Palmer co-edited the magazine *Joglars* with the Clark Coolidge, a poet who is socially and aesthetically connected with many of the writers featured in this book. The early 1960s proved to be a pivotal period, in which Palmer met some of the writers who were to influence his poetics—Robert Duncan, Robert Creeley, and Louis Zukofsky.

After graduating from Harvard, Palmer lived in Europe for a couple of years and studied at the University of Florence. He moved back to the United States in 1969 and settled in San Francisco. Since that time, Palmer has taught at Brown University, the University of Chicago, and the University of California, San Diego. He has also undertaken collaborations with visual artists (Gerhard Richter, Irving Petlin, and Sandro Chia) and choreographers (Margaret Jenkins).

Palmer's poetry resists description: it is idea-centered, disjunctive, and non-narrative on the one hand, and sensual, gestural, and surreal on the other. In Palmer's work these approaches are not at odds. Like some of the other poets in this book, he eschews narrative order out of a belief that such order can disguise more than it reveals. In fact, many of Palmer's supposedly "non-narrative" techniques contain as much in-depth emotional and psychological information as a more recognizably narrative poem.

One of the first things you will notice about Palmer's work is the emphasis on the aural. In a sequence of poems dedicated to Robert Duncan, Palmer wrote: "You can bring down a house with sound." The poem ends: "Rain came in. / Noises not ours." Palmer's poetry challenges conventional notions of authorship by consistently integrating sounds and voices "not ours." In an interview with Keith Tuma,

Palmer noted : "I'm very conscious of the role that poetry can play as resistant to and as a critique of the discourse of power by undermining assumptions about meaning and univocality." Palmer's poems are never propagandistic or hortatory, however. For those who are new to his work, I might recommend reading Palmer's poetry along with that of earlier politically-engaged poets—notably Kenneth Patchen and Charles Reznikoff, who wrote about political issues using complex and often elliptical speakers. You could also read Palmer's work in company with Bernadette Mayer's *Utopia* and Fanny Howe's work to appreciate the variety of methods by which poets incorporate political concerns and philosophical inquiry into their writing.

Palmer is the author of numerous books of poetry, including *Codes Appearing: Poems 1979–1988* (New Directions, 2001), *The Promises of Glass* (New Directions, 2000), *The Lion Bridge: Selected Poems 1972–1995* (New Directions, 1998), *First Figure* (North Point, 1984), *Notes for Echo Lake* (North Point, 1981), and *Without Music* (Black Sparrow, 1977). I suggest you start with *The Lion Bridge* and then work your way back to the original collections. "The collections are unique," writes critic Lauri Ramey, "and each of a piece: the elegant play of silent spaces in *Without Music* counterpoints the social and performantive character of *First Figure*; the 'insane clairty' of the cacophonic voices in *Sun* resonates against the hyper-linguistic autobiography of *Notes for Echo Lake*."

[Song of the Round Man]

for Sarah when she's older

The round and sad-eyed man puffed cigars as if
he were alive. Gillyflowers
to the left of the apple, purple bells to the right

and a grass-covered hill behind.
I am sad today said the sad-eyed man
for I have locked my head in a Japanese box

and lost the key.
I am sad today he told me
for there are gillyflowers by the apple

and purple bells I cannot see.
Will you look at them for me
he asked, and tell me what you find?

I cannot I replied
for my eyes have grown sugary and dim
from reading too long by candlelight.

Tell me what you've read then
said the round and sad-eyed man.
I cannot I replied

for my memory has grown tired and dim
from looking at things that can't be seen
by any kind of light

and I've locked my head in a Japanese box
and thrown away the key.
Then I am you and you are me

said the sad-eyed man as if alive.
I'll write you in where I should be
between the gillyflowers and the purple bells

and the apple and the hill
and we'll puff cigars from noon till night
as if we were alive.

[interview]

Daniel Kane: We began our interview before September 11th, and the questions I asked you then strike me now as oddly ridiculous. Could you offer any reflections on the state of poetry in the aftermath of the attack?

Michael Palmer: *The New York Times* reports that a young child being led to shelter from his school, upon seeing the falling bodies, remarked to his teacher something like, "Look, the birds are on fire." A friend and visual artist, Hanna Hannah, just back from Paris, told me of her conversation in the taxi to the airport with her driver, a man from Guinea, who said of the terrorists, "*Ils sont allés au bout de l'imagination.*" ("They have traveled to the limits of the imagination." Or perhaps, "the imaginable.")

What followed in the ensuing days was what the poet Robert Hass has described, I think quite accurately, as "the hijacking of the disaster" by the extreme right. One of the first casualties of this second terrifying moment was, as ever, language itself. My thoughts inevitably returned to the days of the Vietnam War, the time of "peacekeeper missiles," "pacification" programs, and destroying the village to save it—the discourse of power mobilizing against meaning.

We lived then, it's accurate to say, within a world of manipulated and destabilized reference. But the truth is that the linguistic field is never entirely stable, and that it is a source both of great danger and great poetic possibility. Poetry itself, when it is more than verse and more than a display of creative cleverness, is also a dangerous place, a site of slippages and folds, of irrational commands from the *melos,* where a multiplicity of meanings may be joined in a word, and where the *nothing* beneath is never far from the surface—a place, in other words, where the arbitrary and the necessary play out an intense negotiation concerning the possible.

DK: Can you give an example of a poem that is "more than verse" and how it might function in the face of catastrophe?

MP: The remark I quote above by Hass occurred during his introduction to a reading that Lyn Hejinian, Forrest Hamer, Jewelle Gomez, Bob, and I gave to celebrate the opening of a bookstore in San Francisco on Friday the 14th. We chose to read poems of our own along with poems by other poets associated with the city (and undoubtedly, we all had the moment in mind).

Thinking of my daughter so close to the event, and of being so far from her, I read section 29 of George Oppen's *Of Being Numerous,* moved always by George's sense of the one and the many, the thought of being numerous, the question of being numerous, the idea of being numerous. I also read a poem by Robert Duncan, "The Sentinels," from his final volume, *Ground Work II: In the Dark.* It is one of his "dream descent" poems, a poem of after-light and ghost folk, images brought back from sleep, of creatures witness to our transitoriness, our darkness.

We all remarked later how unusually attentive the audience was that evening, as if poetry mattered a bit more in such circumstances, or its purposes were clearer given its attention to matters of living and dying and even laughter, of which there was some. I remember writing to the Mexican poet Pura López Colomé after the reading that on such occasions people listen to poetry differently, with greater permission for the logic of its music and greater permission for its difficulties.

Finally, for whatever reasons, I've found myself returning to Wallace Stevens's final collection, *The Rock*:

> It is an illusion that we were ever alive,
> Lived in the houses of mothers, arranged ourselves
> By our own motions in a freedom of air.

And also to Paul Schmidt's heroically unrealizable translations of Velimir Khlebnikov:

> I'm going out again today
> into life, into the marketplace,
> to lead a regiment of songs
> against the roar of rat and race.

DK: Can poetry have a political impact in the United States if it caters to a relatively limited, privileged audience?

MP: A poetry of instrumental rhetoric—such as some of Amiri Baraka's, or some of Pablo Neruda's, or some of Nazim Hikmet's and Aimé Césaire's, or some of Vladimir Mayakovsky's, or some of Allen Ginsberg's and Adrienne Rich's—aims to incite to action. It is directed outward, and is direct rather than indirect (though exactly *how* direct might be worth exploring in detail). It speaks for an imagined many, with whom the author identifies in terms of utopian aspirations. It is the poetry we properly think of first when considering explicitly political verse.

However, poetry as critique—as a critique of power—exists in many forms. Anna Akhmatova's refusal to efface her erotic subjectivity was a real enough critique to draw significant attention and concern from Stalin, in a nation where poetry was known very much to matter. The complexly visceral lyric experiments of César Vallejo must be read within the tumultuous field of his political consciousness. When Robert Creeley read his intensely personal and innovative early lyrics at large political demonstrations against the Vietnam War, we felt their appropriateness alongside more public verse.

To understand the resistant effects of poetry, it is probably most convenient to consider those totalitarian societies where it is prohibited or strictly controlled, and many have done so. Yet we must look inward, too, toward the censorship of the marketplace, fully supported by our supine media, for the regulation and surveillance of poetry within our own culture. To cite a ludicrously blatant example, we have only to turn to *The New York Times Book Review,* where, on the rare occasions it does review poetry, only the blandest of pap receives a "safe for consumption" label. It is not really so far from that to the robotic and shamelessly simplistic speech of our forty-third President, the one who was not elected, the one who is a poetry-free zone unto himself, and who would seem, at least initially, to have a free hand to direct our response to the monstrous crimes of September 11th. I fear that no terrorist could wish for more, but I deeply hope I will be proven wrong, just as I hope that the flag will not be manipulated as it has been in the past to sanction anti-constitutional measures and the murderous abuse of force.

Poetry in the United States, as in many cultures, does have a limited audience, but it is not exclusively a privileged one. I think that an audience is drawn to the space of poetry for the way in which words there may operate, and images circulate, so as to offer an alternative to discourse as usual and to thought as usual, an alternative to the learned logic of our daily duties and negotiations. That role for poetry—and it is one of critique among many other things—is as old as the art and the *polis* both; yet it is only sustainable through the radical renewal of that art. If poetry too tests the limits of the imaginable, it is in service to the expansion of thought, rather than its annihilation.

DK: Your idea of "the radical renewal of that art" suggests that the very act of innovation is inherently revolutionary. It reminds me of something Charlie Haden of the Liberation Music Orchestra said in an interview. Asked if he wished jazz musicians would generally be more politically active, Haden explained that the very act of creating innovative jazz was political and liberating, so that further commitment wasn't really an issue for him. Does that make sense to you as a poet who doesn't write in a way that—as you say of Ginsberg and Rich—is directed "outward"?

MP: I think there is a great deal of sense in what Haden says, though naturally not all would agree. One can certainly defend the notion of protopolitical or protodialectical meaning in work that is not overtly political. Let's put it this way, anyone who can play like that must know something.

I would agree with part of what you say concerning avant-garde practices, though to call them "inherently revolutionary" seems overstated. The historical vanguards took many forms, of course. Among a certain number of the Italian Futurists, such as Filippo Marinetti, there was a strong identification with fascism. The same for the Vorticists in England, who briefly took on the coloring of vanguardism. And we should add that some of the most politically progressive poets in the twentieth century chose to work in traditional forms. So in considering the inside/outside status of poetry, and the consequences for a culture of its apparent inconsequentiality, we must avoid the temptation to find one-to-one correspondences. Poetry does not need to justify itself, in fact cannot justify itself, by means of exaggerated or inappropriate claims.

DK: Despite the fact that many of your poems challenge the concept of stable reference, I sense that you still hold the old-fashioned and powerful idea of the poet as inspired vessel.

MP: As far as the muse goes, perhaps she had better be given a rest. Rough handling has tattered her garments. On a thousand occasions she has been asked to inspire but not herself to respire. She has been conceived to exist without breath of her own, while rendering it to others. She expires, that the afflatus may exist. Enough of such slaughter.

 Nonetheless, there is always an outside that brings us words, and an other with whom we speak. Without this conversation, a two-way conversation, there is no poem. Fernando Pessoa writes of the poet as a *resonateur* of multiple tones and forces, inner and outer. Its current theoretical disrepute aside, the "linguistic turn" in philosophy, insofar as it speaks to poetry, can also be seen as contributing to a rather ancient notion of a primary engagement with language or *logos*.

DK: In your poem "Lens," you write, "I failed to draw a map and you followed it perfectly / because the word for 'cannot' inscribes itself here." The word *cannot* seems to arrive precisely from this "outside" that the author doesn't so much control as administrate. Is there joy in denying control over language's presence on the page?

MP: Administration is for administrators, those who manage things or in certain instances impose things. There are poets who work that way, but I don't think we have to consider them. What, in my experience, do poets do? We wait for things, we watch and listen for things, we steal things, somewhat like magpies; and then again we shape things and make things.

So much goes into poetry, so much that may seem paradoxical—intuition, judgment, choice, chance, construction, rage, desire, self, non-self, dream, reason, the unconscious, etc.—that the question of authorial control becomes itself an ungovernable one. Ungovernable, that is, unless we make the answer, the definition, hopelessly reductive. Yet when we acknowledge that, we have at least taken a step toward understanding poetry's multiple natures and possibilities.

Another paradox: There is inevitably an essential element of subversion in enduring work, subversion of expectation about the subject, about the line, about caesura, the pause, about the turn, about what follows, about the end, about belief and the breath and the step. Yet this is a subversiveness we expect and demand if we ask of poetry something more than a vignette in verse, or metered homilies. And since the time of Plato we have praised and demonized its strangeness, its estrangement, and there will always be those among us who would banish it from their republics. This returns us to that question of control, though perhaps in a different sense than you first intended. All compelling poetry itself is an *ungovernable* entity, whether it be composed in traditional or freer forms. You might say that it is a site that resists surveillance.

DK: In your book *Notes for Echo Lake,* I'm struck by the wide range of forms you employ—there are prose poems, highly rhythmic poems, abstract fragments. Yet I'm struck especially by those poems that seem to evoke nursery rhymes or fables. Could you talk about your relationship to the fable by discussing your motivation for writing "Song of the Round Man"?

MP: "Song of the Round Man" is the first in a cycle of poems for my daughter, begun when she was first coming into language, that moment when the poetic possibility of language is not yet estranged from the practical or the instrumental. It is a stage when language resembles a kind of magical practice. Both nursery rhyme and fable access and evoke such linguistic powers, the one by incantation, the other by fabulistic narration. They open the door onto a world of *a-musement* (Robert Duncan's term) that is perhaps primary to language-as-making.

It is a world I think we must recover (recover, but as something different, of course) as we come into working with words. This cycle was for me part of that job of unforgetting, of anamnesia. I was also eager to see whether such songs were still possible without falling into triteness, whether in such a time as ours rhyme in all its dimensions could still be honored.

DK: Why might something like rhyme *need* to be honored? That is, what are the conditions in poetry today that impel you to resuscitate or renovate traditional poetic and narrative structures instead of forging ahead and continuing to, as Pound advised, "make it new"?

MP: I was using the term metaphorically, thinking of its derivation from the Latin *rhythmus.* Etymological speculation has it that the word may ultimately derive from an Indo-European sign for the arm—more specifically the arm extended, as in dance. Cooper's *Thesaurus* of 1565 offers us: "*Rhythmus,* number or harmonie in speakying; meeter; rhyme." So, I was speaking—or speakying—of the play of identity and difference, harmonies and disharmonies, that occurs at so many levels of the poem, and that is at once ancient, at the origins of the lyric, and entirely new. "Make it new," for Pound, was certainly a modernist call to arms, a call for new forms. Yet Pound's teachers in that art were Dante and Cavalcanti, Homer, Sappho, Propertius and Catullus, Li Po, Arnaut Daniel and François Villon, Théophile Gautier, Arthur Rimbaud, Browning, and Yeats, among many others.

The urge to innovation without that ground (I mean, of course, some version of one's own, particular to one's cultural needs, and not necessarily so vast) can easily become superficial, a novelty act or fashion show. To "rhyme" things, to create a field of rhyme (I'm thinking here at once of sound and meaning), at least has the potential to be a profoundly dialectal activity. In this regard, Pound emphasized attention to "the tone-leading of vowels" as necessary to the poem's coherence.

DK: In "Song of the Round Man," the sad-eyed man says, "I am you and you are me" and "I'll write you in where I should be." It seems that the presence of the author here is being fractured by the very act of writing—that is, writing appears to provoke absence as opposed to presence.

MP: I'm not sure I've ever actually met the author. The author passes through my life, a kind of presence/absence, but we do not speak. Maybe I get an occasional glimpse in dreams, those not of falling towers, but he/she never joins me for morning coffee. When I go to the market or roam the streets, I will sometimes imagine a tap on the shoulder, or hear a whisper, but when I turn around no one is there. If I knew the author, I might better be able to find him/her in the work.

On the other hand, I will occasionally find myself in the work, lurking somewhat guiltily in the author's place. On such occasions, my instinct is to depart as quietly as possible, but this isn't always easy to do. Sometimes the exit signs have been removed, or the instructions for egress appear in a language that is mysterious to me. Occasionally I will reach the door only to find that it has been sealed shut, possibly by the author. Sometimes I wonder whether it is the author who occasionally causes my reading glasses to break or my watch to stop. Sometimes I suspect that there might be many more than one.

Lewis Warsh

Feelings of love were impai

I put in my order for the

& the holidays are "u

You can wear the same

She complains that sh
beautiful while h
wore yesterday f
bother washing

*l*ewis warsh

was born in the Bronx in 1944. His parents were high school teachers. Warsh attended Bronx High School of Science, where he took a creative writing class with another talented future author (Samuel Delany) and joined a club of precocious bohemians that met Friday evenings to discuss politics, art, and folk music.

In 1966, Warsh graduated from City College of New York. His first job was at the New York City Welfare Department as a caseworker, patrolling the streets of Bush-wick, Brooklyn. By this time, he was living with poet Anne Waldman, and he was a major presence on the Lower East Side poetry scene. In 1968, Warsh moved to Bolinas, California, and lived on the West Coast for a couple of years. Returning to New York City in the 1970s, Warsh and Bernadette Mayer decided to live together, write and edit lots of books and magazines, and start a family. Warsh currently lives in New York and teaches at Long Island University in Brooklyn.

Warsh is often described as a "Second Generation" New York School poet, so I would urge you to read his poems alongside those of the first generation (Ashbery, Koch, O'Hara, and Schuyler) to see how he expands on such New York School writing practices as the list poem, parataxis, collage, and diary. In his most recent writings (particularly in *Avenue of Escape* and *The Origin of the World*), Warsh has developed a distinctive double-spaced, long line that is somewhere between a sentence and a poetic line.

I would also recommend reading Warsh's poetry in conjunction with Mayer's work. (See Mayer's *Midwinter Day* for an inside look at what it was like spending a day in Massachusetts with Lewis and the kids.) And, to appreciate the rebellious elements of his work and life, you could consider Warsh's poetry in relation to that of Allen Ginsberg and Jack Kerouac. Like them, he writes: "I wanted to be free of any restraints, to be able to curse and smoke and have sex without feeling guilty. I was already too introverted—I needed a kind of Dionysian balance." His work certainly reflects this, although the Dionysian is frequently given an Apollonian dose of the daily life.

Warsh's books of poetry and fiction include *The Origin of the World* (Creative Arts, 2001), *Avenue of Escape* (Long News, 1995), and *Information from the Surface of Venus* (United Artists, 1987). If you're new to Warsh's work, I suggest starting with the *Angel Hair Anthology* (Granary Books, 2001) and proceeding to *The Origin of the World*. The former contains excerpts from the issues of *Angel Hair* magazine that Waldman and Warsh edited in the late 1960s and early '70s. By reading this book, you'll get a sense of the poets who influenced Warsh, and vice versa.

[*from* **The Outer Banks**]

People meet on a blind date & eventually get married for the sake
        of discretion ("my parents wanted me to")

You find out what interests you, but don't do it–not yet,
        anyway–since it's more interesting to put it all off
        till tomorrow, to let things slide, to trap the thought
        in its beauty like a tiger in a cage & watch it climb the
        walls & disfigure itself out of sheer helplessness

You map out a theory of knowledge & watch it dissolve like an
        integer divided by itself, but turned on their sides
        the numbers look like songs

You pretend to work hard so others will leave you alone

You talk to strangers & megalomaniacs, you read books you
        read before

You prefer pieces of paper with words on them to people, but
        that phase passes

You identify with the tree outside your window: all my family
        makes a home here but the branches are obscure, even
        to me

You sing a judicious symphony like a necklace of amber beads

[interview]

Daniel Kane: The poems in *The Origin of the World* quietly evoke both a "you" and an "I," and the two subjects are often conflated to the point where, as a reader, one doesn't know if one is being addressed directly or being told a story. Could you talk about your use of the "I" and the "you"? Are they interchangeable, and if so, why?

Lewis Warsh: In most cases the "I" and the "you" can be read interchangeably. Often I write "you" when I'm addressing myself, giving myself advice, but the reader can take it in a more generalized way, so the "you" can be everyone. What I'm aiming for, every time I use one pronoun or another, is a multiplicity of possibilities. I want to encompass as many points of view as possible. In the last line of "The Outer Banks," the "you" ("you are my shadow") is definitely "the other."

DK: What are some ways a novice writer might think about subjectivity—and using pronoun shifts—in his or her own poetry?

LW: Working with secrets is a good way of approaching subjective material. There's always another layer to work your way through; it just goes on forever. No one knows how anyone actually thinks about anything. This might be one starting point: to look at your thought process as a kind of "secret" world, what makes you different from anyone else, and the ultimate source of your poetry. This might be as mundane as the "quandariness" Frank O'Hara experiences in "The Day Lady Died," the thwarted expectancy in Ted Berrigan's "Personal Poem," or the basic feeling of loss in a poem like Kenneth Koch's "To Marina."

    Once you start dealing with subjective experience, the poem will dictate its own form. The first poems I ever wrote, at age thirteen or fourteen, were straightforward emotional statements. It took a while to realize that simply saying "I love you" wasn't enough. Then for many years I refused to use "I" in a poem. I felt more comfortable with "he" or "you" when I really meant myself. Not everyone wants to write subjectively, and you have to be careful, as a teacher, to present it simply as an option. Many people prefer going about writing as if they were in hiding.

DK: Now that you've brought up form—echoing, it seems to me, Robert Creeley's idea that form is an extension of content—I'm very interested in the form your lines take in *The Origin of the World*. Was the distinction between poetry and prose useful to you, and is *The Origin of the World* a kind of hybrid prose-poetry form?

LW: I'm a fiction writer as well as a poet, so I think my attraction to this hybrid form is that I can write in both sentences and lines at the same time. The poems feel narrative to me, like a work of fiction, but the individual sections feel like lines of poetry. What I wanted is a form where I wasn't confined to either/or, where I could break down the boundaries between poetry and fiction, where I could include all my impulses towards writing with as few restrictions as possible. After writing for thirty or so years, I wanted a place where a feeling of absolute freedom was available to me, as much as that's possible. When there are two possibilities—in this case, poetry and prose—that means there's a third possibility. Two always leads to three, like having a baby. Two always implies a synthesis, something unknown. The actual act of writing these poems was like taking a step across some imaginary boundary line into a space I didn't know about before, a genre-less space that doesn't have a name.

DK: It's interesting that you talk about a "genre-less space," as the borders between poetry and prose in *The Origin of the World* are so wonderfully porous. In your poem "The Outer Banks," the third-to-last stanza breaks lines more resolutely than in all the other stanzas. How conscious were you of the lineation and lyricism in the lines:

> —could
> anyone of them, or you, predict
> this spell of cold weather
> we've been having recently?

LW: The section you refer to is the longest in the book. "The Outer Banks" was the first of these poems, and I gave myself license to break the mold and actually include what looks like a poem—instead of just writing in lines or fragments. The Outer Banks, by the way, is this actual place on the coast of North Carolina that juts out into the ocean further than any place along the Eastern coastline.

DK: Yeah, I spent a number of lovely days bicycling through those Outer Banks. At points I could see the ocean on either side of me!

LW: The title is meant to evoke the question: How far out can you go? The section you refer to is the climactic moment, the point where the poem evolves into a love poem in which the "other" is always present, if only in the form of a shadowy presence cast by the light of a candle. Again, I wasn't interested in restrictions. The fact that many of the fragments are purposefully flat doesn't mean that I had to deny myself a kind of lyric voice from time to time. Longing for the absent other, which is the central feeling of all the poems, always lends itself to lyricism. It's why so many of the lines are abbreviated, why each line is like a new beginning. It's like I'm stumbling around in the dark, looking for someone who isn't there.

DK: Were there any models for *The Origin of the World*?

LW: I like the idea of "a thousand plateaus," which is the title of a book by Gilles Deleuze and Felix Guattari, in which they say, at some point, that "every book is an assemblage." So one can think of these lines as horizon lines stretching out to nowhere, or an outcrop of plateaus—places that just kind of level off, one after another. The poems grow out of a sense of accumulation—in this case what seems like random lines—but the real pleasure, for me, is in the arrangement. The lines in the finished poem are never in the same order as when I first wrote them. I often have to discard a lot of material that doesn't fit. Collage plays a big role—disparate units side by side. When I first started writing these poems I was very excited that I could do something I hadn't done before, that was neither poetry or prose. I've always liked reading fragmented philosophical works, in which you could stop and start anew every few lines, and where the process was more important than any main idea. The late movies of Rudy Burckhardt (all his variations, his use of music, his humor, the way he spirals between images) were important to me. I try to think like a movie editor: each line is a frame. Much of what influences me are works in media other than poetry.

DK: What do you mean by "the absent other"?

LW: Of course it's a person. The blank page on which one writes one's poem is a stand-in for the person who isn't there. The truth of that statement is a whole life story. So you can say that writing a poem is a way of making something present that isn't there. The poem is the illusory link with the other. It gives me a lot of incentive to make the poem really good because it has to bring the absent person into being. It has to create its own presence.

DK: In a way, the poems in your book generate more of a mood than a narrative or paraphrasable ideas. Were you influenced by any specific musical idea, e.g., the tone poem? I ask you this because of the line "When I was thirteen I got up on a stage in a house of God (so called) & sang a song whose meaning the meaning of which was in the inflections of the words." (This from your poem "Avenue of Escape.")

LW: That was my first reading: my bar mitzvah! I had to get up in front of an audience and sing a very lengthy song in Hebrew, which I had memorized, without knowing what any of the words meant. What I was taught were the inflections; the way I sang conveyed the real meaning. It wasn't necessary to know what the words actually meant. The English dictionary, in this sense, is a very romantic work—the idea that words have equal-signs that link them with what they mean. Like Hebrew, Chinese is a sound-based language—the same word can mean four different things depending on how you say it.

I talk a lot about music with my students, about how someone like Miles Davis or Bill Evans or Billie Holiday is creating a sound that is undeniably his or her own. It seems to be coming directly from them and no one else. After a while, when I write, that's the sound I listen for—the sound that I trust, the one closest to what I think of as "my own." Sometimes it's hard to get in touch with that sound, and then I write something else that might be interesting in another way. There's a way of going against your sound that can lead to something exciting. Jackson Pollock wasn't going to wake up and paint any other way than the way he figured out how to do. That was his way. It takes years sometimes to even approach the possibility of discovering a music that makes sense. I tend to think that the poems in *The Origin of the World* and my books of fiction and all my other books of poems all have the same sound. *The Origin of the World* has a very definite signature because it's written in a specific form, but it's really no different from everything else I've written.

DK: The way you talk about music and sound suggests you have a relatively stable or even organic conception of identity or lyric voice. When you say "the sound that I trust, the one closest to what I think of as 'my own,'" I take it to mean that you imagine a natural voice in writing is possible.

LW: My inclination to write in a certain way, as opposed to the way someone else writes, is based on a million factors. "Natural" or "voice" or "natural voice" aren't terms I ever think about. Since no two people write alike, even if they're associated with a so-called "school," one assumes that everyone is writing in a way that merges with who they are. My writing is an extension of myself. It isn't an intellectual exercise, or a didactic statement of what I think all writing should be. I'm interested in a lot of writers who write very differently than I do, and I'm interested in making a bridge to the real, whatever that is—between me and something. I have this authority problem—meaning as "author" I don't want to be told what to do. When I read a poem, I then identify a certain way of writing with the author, as if it were the same thing. Identity is often slippery, and the way I write may be only synonymous with who I am at that moment. I think about this question a lot, but when I'm writing I just forget it.

DK: Love is melancholy in these poems. I'm thinking now of a line from your poem "Entering Night": "My father went into the hallway & began calling for the police to save him from my mother whom he didn't recognize & whom he thought wanted to murder him & steal his money." How do you deal with writing students who tend to write of love in entirely positive ways?

LW: Most of the students I've encountered are in touch with their sadness—the absence of the love object and the great romantic tradition. They get this more from song lyrics, which are hardly positive when it comes to defining love, than they do from reading poetry. I don't think my vision of love is particularly bleak. On the contrary, I think these particular poems are about the ways you can step back from your experience, to look at the unhappiness from a distance. They're about resiliency. Real bleakness would mean that you're drowning, that you're going under. It's one thing to stare into the abyss—being in it, with no way out, isn't a place I ever want to go.

DK: Could you talk about the preponderance of incarceration imagery in your poem "Avenue of Escape"?

LW: I'm alluding to daily life. "90 Are Arrested in Inquiry into Internet Child-Sex Ring." That's a headline in today's paper. The world is set up so people can live multiple lives, which is one reason why writing about one's secrets might be important. The idea of imprisonment is more than a metaphor—the idea of being locked in, anywhere, is unthinkable. The idea of punishing anyone, the way it's done, doesn't make sense, whether it's the Taliban idea of cutting off the hand of the thief or the idea of solitary confinement, where you're allowed a half-hour of exercise each day. Capital punishment, life sentences without parole—all this has been around a long time and it hasn't stopped people from committing crimes. At the same time, most people are locked into prisons of their own. The body is a prison and there's no way out. The mind is definitely a prison, but there's a lot of space in it, too, if you know where to go. People punish themselves for crimes they didn't even commit. Get into the possible mind-set of someone sitting in a prison cell and you realize that person is you. Issues of transgression—all the subjects I include in "Avenue of Escape"—are on my mind all the time. I have a feeling that the world is a lot darker than anything I know.

Marjorie Welish

...or enclosing struct...

...tering or enclosing struc...

...a lid is typically incomplet...

...phases

...g in multiples" readily mod...

...ngured, may be recon...

...ural reduction in...

marjorie welish

was born in New York City in 1944. Welish remembers her father reading passages from classical history or a line of poetry aloud to her on a regular basis. By secondary school, the cultural cosmopolitanism assumed by her parents—who sought out lectures, concerts, and museum exhibitions, often bringing her along—was set. Welish studied at New York's Hunter High School, and recalls that her English teacher sent students to hunt for favorite poems to be discussed in class. Welish transferred to Brooklyn Friends School, a school that typically taught college-level courses to adolescents: Chaucer, Spenser, Milton, Shakespeare, etc. Other early influences included W. H. Auden, whose poem "Musée des Beaux Arts" widened her awareness of a poetry sophisticated in both subject and tone. Lewis Carroll's *Alice in Wonderland* and his verse parodies were also instrumental in informing Welish's poetics. Perhaps indicating a potential source for the lyric impulses in her work, Welish notes that hearing psalms and hymns, together with madrigals, folk songs, and some blues, all fed into her love of language.

A painter and art critic as well as a poet—her paintings are represented by the Baumgartner Gallery and the Aaron Galleries—Welish currently lives in New York City and teaches at the Pratt Institute in Brooklyn. She has also served as a visiting art critic and poetry professor at Brown University. Of teaching, Welish states, "Teaching gives me sanction to read and to think—a constantly amazing blessing. Whether I teach an immersion course in the poetry and poetics of a certain writer (such as Stevens), a course devoted to the problematic of the lyric, or alternatively a seminar in the social history and theory of criticism, it is all generative of writing I myself do."

Like many avant-garde writers today, Welish has credited living in a city—New York City in particular—with affecting her poetics. She once told me that "the urban 'experience' as a cultural instrumentality is a condition for creativity that I assume, even presuppose, especially given the simultaneities and intensities of differing events that attach themselves to ideas we have of modernity—by now a commonplace in literature. For my sense of literature, the poetics of the city is companionable; the city as locale is less persuasive." Such a take on the city helps us align Welish's work with the poetry of Ashbery, Lauterbach, and others.

Welish's books of poetry include *The Annotated "Here" and Selected Poems* (Coffee House, 2000), *Casting Sequences* (University of Georgia, 1993), and *The Windows Flew Open* (Burning Deck, 1991). If you're new to Welish's work, I suggest starting with the *The Annotated "Here" and Selected Poems.* Note how music and art serve as recurrent subjects in Welish's poetry, particularly in the selections from *Casting Sequences,* which detail her fascination with objectifying and abstracting language even when it functions as a mode of description. Decidedly non-autobiographical on the surface, Welish meditates on spatial and sensual intensity in much of her poetry, and in reading her we really get a feeling for how the mind can move, loop, and stretch in all sorts of lush and complicated ways.

[This Near That]

Imagine a logic of like size
arresting exteriors, even as interiors are restless

skeptical, or defective relative to use
as a reservoir, aqueduct, or kiosk.

"A small simple sheltering or enclosing structure."
A locale requiring a lid is logically incomplete.

A definition of pluses
"and occurring in multiples" readily modular

if verbally reconfigured, may be reconfigured
as follows: "a structural reduction in answer to Tatlin."

Across a wall is a something
Something designates a wall.

"Something having a flat bottom and four upright sides" is a delegate
of sets of descriptions. Our professed subject.

Daniel Kane: I am oddly moved by the combined language of geometry and emotion in your poem "This Near That." Could you tell us something about how you came to write the poem?

Marjorie Welish: "This Near That" is one of four related poems devoted to the problem of defining an abstract object. Each of the four poems arrives at a somewhat different notion of what this object is, given that our language is a creative instrument which interprets as much as it explains. Each of the poems, then, engages the difficulty of arriving at definitions when interpretive description is all language has at its disposal.

DK: What then is the role of the imagination in determining what an object is?

MW: Real definitions seek the essential nature of something. The imagination, being a speculative tool, explores the more tenuous aspects of definitions, as you have said. It is not shy about inventing as well as exploring definitions through language; indeed, it is through language and its imaginative exploits that the chimera by which things "are" comes about.

DK: William Carlos Williams famously said, "No ideas but in things." You appear to be moving away from this belief, instead suggesting that the opposite is true: that ideas are what determine the very "thingness" of things. Does this make sense to you in light of this poem and your overall poetics?

MW: Yes. Sense data have been largely overrated. This having been said, the cultural value of putting our ideological or expressive clichés to the test by observing matters firsthand provides us with crucial help in gauging the weaknesses of ideas.

DK: Is "This Near That" a challenge to "objective" truth? The title seems to suggest that things only exist in relationship to each other.

MW: It's true, contextual definitions do tend to emphasize the relative claims being made. "This Near That" does presuppose an object of an expanded modern kind, not one presumed to be confined to a single portable thing. The poetic object has long been construed as a sequence, group, field, even a heap—an order of some kind for which interrelations matter, or, at least, matter more than the objects themselves.

DK: You mention the "abstract object." What is it? Your poem reminds me of Sol LeWitt's squares, which are formally abstract yet nevertheless exist materially—in your words, "A small simple sheltering or enclosing structure."

MW: First, I want to thank you for waiting to ask me to identify that thing, that portable thing to which in some sense the poem refers. What the poem is decidedly not about is creating a verbal resemblance to a visual art object. But it does make a certain use of ekphrasis by noting the logical disposition of the work. The object in question is the logical description (together with the functional description) of a box. If that is a thing, you are welcome to it!

Now it happens that a box is commonplace, and because of its ordinariness we erroneously assume it to be simple. But in what sense? Do we assume it to be simple if it has few moving parts? That is to say, is it emotionally or intellectually simple because its technology is elementary? Perhaps the object is complex, despite basic appearance, despite its familiarity.

DK: If a box is not simple, then what is? If the answer is "nothing," then might we start conceiving of your poetic project as working for a kind of rejection of closure—a mimetic of our fragmentary, constantly shifting world?

MW: Let me answer you this way. As I mentioned, "This Near That" is only one of four related poems clustered around definitions and descriptions of a box. The three related poems—"A Work," "The Open," and "'This Hit That' and the Like"—suggest a field of inquiry more than a fixed designation. This is appropriate to considering the nature of a thing, and the aggregated instances of inquiry themselves substitute a poetic object for the commodity. In other words, critical thought in lyric, I would argue, demolishes the commodity.

Vladimir Tatlin was a Russian avant-garde artist, a Productivist. Believing that art is useless, he sought to make artifacts that were useful. The words quoted in the poem are my own: I am citing myself writing a piece of art criticism as I engage the notion of the box as useful and useless, by turns.

DK: Well, you've anticipated my question: Who or what is Tatlin? I ask you this both because I'm honestly curious and because I'd like to be able to answer my students, who ask, "Why should I read a poem that requires me to do research?" Are there ways for teachers of poetry to show students that *not* knowing all of the references in a poem doesn't negate the experience or the pleasure?

MW: Your question is a direct challenge to a poetics that thrives on poetry-as-theory. It is a valid question, of course. But first let me frame it by saying that in the history of ideas, Romanticism dominates certain approaches. With the teaching of the poetry of the New York School, for instance, "experience" and "pleasure" are code words for "anti-classicizing" (or "free from academic style"). These are unexamined assumptions, about which the New York School became very self-conscious. Think of Frank O'Hara's catalogue of proper names, including "Ghana," "Richmond Lattimore," "Patsy," "Bonnard" and "New World Writing," all in his poem "The Day Lady Died," or elsewhere—"Bauhaus," "Mayakovsky." O'Hara is putting the avant-garde on the same footing as the here-and-now. That these poems name art or poetry obscure to some readers is not a worry. This is a poetry for which modernities are common knowledge and may be taken for granted in this context. The same with Tatlin.

The self-consciousness of New York School poetry, meanwhile, loves to expose experience and pleasure as cliché. Gustave Flaubert has much to say about this. His *Dictionary of Received Ideas* is both documentary and parody of what passes for authenticity in firsthand experience. So academic or clichéd are our experiences that taking them at face value is quite suspect.

We tell ourselves that knowledge is useful, and so cannot be made aesthetic. The *Iliad* is a defiant example of this, since it is an epic precisely designed to make conventional knowledge memorable. How to treat a stranger, and with what protocols and hospitality; how to embalm a body; how to forge a shield—all of this cultural knowledge finds determinant beauty in the poem.

DK: I know you've taught writing in various colleges here in New York. You've probably run in to quite a few students who believe poetry is entirely about self-expression. How do you encourage your students to develop an individual style that combines self-expression with attention to ideas and language?

MW: By concentrating on an assignment. The curious effect of engaging an assignment and of rejecting merely proficient results is that singularity manifests itself, and with it, a specificity of tone. I too have met massive resistance when assigning students—college students—to write a poem that conveys a procedure or process. Kicking and screaming all the way, students came up with some good stuff nonetheless, and at least one poem from this assignment has entered the public readings I now do.

DK: I taught an "Introduction to Poetry" class at a community college in Brooklyn this past semester, and it struck me that the majority of students believed that all poetry had to be like Robert Frost (don't get me wrong, though—I actually love Frost!), that every poem has to have a clear message. Were you critiquing Frost when you wrote, "Across a wall is a something / Something designates a wall." It seems you're referring to Frost's famous poem "Mending Wall."

MW: No, these lines are not referring to Frost's poem. They are, once again, referring to descriptions that name something. Thwarting the assumption that all poems "contain symbolism" is a challenge. A very credible poetics, the symbol system (used by Frost and others) demonstrates to the skeptics that a poem is as worthy as prose. The symbolic poem is also a good place to begin to read for poetics. If I follow you correctly, you are trying to convince students trained to identify symbols that other creative poetics are as worthy.

DK: Yes. I guess my problem with "the symbol system," as you call it, is that it encourages a kind of medicalized view of reader-reception—that is, you look *into* the poem to discover how it works. Reading a poem for its symbolic meaning might diminish the value one could place on poetic surface (surface in this case meaning the aural sheen of a poem). Do you distinguish in your classes between "meaning" and "surface"?

MW: Saying that a symbolic poem presents a valid poetics to an inexperienced reader of poetry is not to say that I endorse symbolism. One can identify the rhetoric of a statement without being persuaded by it! One can recognize and teach poetics of poetry not one's own—or rather, one should be able to be objective in this way. Paul Celan is the Robert Frost of my workshop called "The Lyric Lately," not because Celan produces a symbolic poem like Frost, but precisely because he doesn't. And students with expectations of encountering poems in the manner of Celan are startled to learn that Michael Palmer has been reading Celan, and writing poems through the meaning of Celan without the manner. Meanwhile, I have taught my students some Mallarmé, in whose work surface and depth, music and meaning, are always co-present.

Remember that our discussion here is much more abstract than it would be in a classroom. I've taught elementary school kids the poetics of Yeats and of Williams—without their knowing it. In other words, a teacher can embed theory in practice.

DK: How would you go about discussing poetry without resorting to "interpreting" or "defining" the essential meaning of a poem?

MW: Given that in both my poetry and my pedagogy textual strategies are so crucial, I tend to teach a spectrum of several very strong poetics for which the strategy is marked. Of these, the paradigms for "definition" shift widely. For some, the very notion of "definition" is anathema. I recall a workshop I taught at Brown University, not devoted to the lyric, in which I asked students to write a poem describing a procedure. I asked them to consider procedures in a certain passage from the *Iliad,* and then write their own.

DK: These questions make me think that there is another tradition of poetry—specifically, sound poetry or concrete poetry—that appears to be in direct opposition to the symbol-based approach. Have you ever taught writers like Hugo Ball or Jackson Mac Low in your classes, and if so, what was that like?

MW: Teaching the sound poetry of John Taggart from the principle of difference within repetition allows me to help the class concentrate on the specific lexical choices that put Taggart's lyric in oral display. Through this, Taggart brings forth a meditative lyric very different from the sonorities and the aesthetic nonsense so finely wrought by Kenward Elmslie, whose performances are directly linked to cabaret. Sound poetries are very much part of my teaching.

DK: Say a teacher came up to you and said, "Marjorie Welish, I'd love to discuss your poem 'This Near That' with my students. How might I begin?" What would be your response?

MW: The teacher might ask: "What are the creative implications for possible worlds in which only definitions exist or only descriptions exist?"

[select bibliography]

Primary Sources

Armantrout, Rae. *Made to Seem*. Los Angeles: Sun & Moon Press, 1995.
————. *Necromance*. Los Angeles: Sun & Moon Press, 1991.
————. *Precedence*. Providence, R.I.: Burning Deck Press, 1985.
————. *The Invention of Hunger*. Berkeley, Calif.: Tuumba Press, 1979.
————. *True*. Berkeley, Calif.: Atelos, 1998.
————. *Veil: New and Selected Poems*. Middletown, Conn.: Wesleyan
    University Press, 2001.

Ashbery, John. *A Wave*. New York: Viking, 1984.
————. *Can You Hear, Bird?* New York: The Noonday Press, 1997.
————. *Chinese Whispers*. New York: Farrar, Straus and Giroux, 2002.
————. *Flow Chart*. New York: Knopf, 1992.
————. *Girls on the Run*. New York: Farrar, Straus and Giroux, 1999.
————. *Houseboat Days*. New York: Penguin, 1977.
————. *One Hundred Multiple-Choice Questions*. New York: Adventures in
    Poetry, 2000.
————. *Other Traditions*. Cambridge, Mass.: Harvard University Press,
    2000.
————. *Self-Portrait in a Convex Mirror*. New York: Penguin, reprint
    edition, 1992.
————. *Shadow Train*. New York: Viking, 1981.
————. *The Mooring of Starting Out: The First Five Books of Poetry*.
    Hopewell, N.J.: The Ecco Press, 1997.
————. *The Tennis Court Oath: A Book of Poems*. Hanover, N.H.: University
    Press of New England, new edition, 1997.
————. *The Vermont Notebook*. New York/Calais, Vt.: Granary Books,
    2001.
————. *Your Name Here*. New York: Farrar, Straus and Giroux, 2000.

Creeley, Robert. *For Love: Poems 1950–1960*. New York: Scribners, 1962.
————. *If I Were Writing This*, New York: New Directions, 2003.
————. *Just in Time: Poems 1984–1994*. New York: New Directions,
    2001.

————. *Later.* New York: New Directions, 1979.

————. *Life & Death.* New York: New Directions, 1998.

————. *Pieces.* New York: Scribners, 1969.

————. *Selected Poems.* Berkeley, Calif.: University of California Press, 1991.

————. *The Collected Poems of Robert Creeley, 1945–1975.* Berkeley, Calif.: University of California Press, 1982.

Howe, Fanny. *Eggs.* Boston: Houghton Mifflin, 1970.

————. *For Erato: The Meaning of Life.* Berkeley, Calif.: Tuumba Press, 1984.

————. *Forged.* Sausalito, Calif.: Post-Apollo Press, 1999.

————. *Introduction to the World.* Great Barrington, Mass.: The Figures, 1986.

————. *One Crossed Out.* St. Paul, Minn.: Graywolf Press, 1997.

————. *Robeson Street.* Farmington, Maine: Alice James Books, 1985.

————. *Selected Poems.* Berkeley, Calif.: University of California Press, 2000.

————. *The End.* Los Angeles: Littoral Books, 1992.

Jarnot, Lisa. *Ring of Fire: Poems.* Cambridge, Mass: Zoland Books, 2001.

————. *Some Other Kind of Mission.* Providence, R.I. Burning Deck Press, 1996.

Koch, Kenneth. *Making Your Own Days: The Pleasures of Reading and Writing Poetry.* Simon & Schuster, 1998.

————. *New Addresses.* New York: Knopf, 2000.

————. *One Train.* New York: Knopf, 1994.

————. *On the Great Atlantic Rainway: Selected Poems 1950–1988.* New York: Knopf, 1994.

————. *A Possible World.* New York: Knopf, 2002.

————. *Sun Out: Selected Poems 1952–1954.* New York: Knopf, 2002.

————. *The Art of Love.* New York: Random House, 1975.

————. *Wishes, Lies, and Dreams.* New York: Harper Perennial, 1999.

Lauterbach, Ann. *And for Example.* New York: Penguin, 1994.

————. *Before Recollection.* Princeton, N.J.: Princeton University Press, 1987.

————. *Clamor*. New York: Penguin, 1992.

————. *If in Time: Selected Poems 1975–2002*. New York: Penguin, 2001.

————. *Many Times, But Then*. Austin: University of Texas Press, 1979.

————. *On a Stair*. New York: Penguin, 1997.

Mayer, Bernadette. *A Bernadette Mayer Reader*. New York: New Directions, 1992.

————. *Another Smashed Pinecone*. Brooklyn, N.Y.: United Artists Books, 1998.

————. *Memory*. Plainfield, Vt.: North Atlantic Books, 1975.

————. *Midwinter Day*. Berkeley, Calif.: Turtle Island Foundation, 1982.

————. *Sonnets*. New York: Tender Buttons, 1989.

————. *Studying Hunger*. New York: Adventures in Poetry, 1975.

————. *The Desires of Mothers to Please Others in Letters*. West Stockbridge, Mass.: Hard Press, 1994.

————. *The Formal Field of Kissing: Translations, Imitations and Epigrams*. New York: Catchword Papers, 1990.

————. *Two Haloed Mourners: Poems*. New York: Granary Books, 1998.

Mullen, Harryette. *Blues Baby: Early Poems*. Lewisburg, Pa.: Bucknell University Press, 2002.

————. *Muse & Drudge*. Philadelphia, Pa.: Singing Horse Press, 1995.

————. *Sleeping with the Dictionary*. Berkeley, Calif.: University of California Press, 2002.

————. *S*PeRM**K*T*. Philadelphia, Pa.: Singing Horse Press, 1992.

————. *Tree Tall Woman: Poems*. Galveston, Tex.: Energy Earth Communications, 1981.

————. *Trimmings*. New York: Tender Buttons, 1991.

Palmer, Michael. *Codes Appearing: Poems 1979–1988*. New York: New Directions, 2001.

————. *Notes for Echo Lake*. San Francisco: North Point Press, 1981.

————. *Sun*. San Francisco: North Point Press, 1988.

————. *The Lion Bridge: Selected Poems, 1972–1995*. New York: New Directions, 1998.

————. *The Promises of Glass*. New York: New Directions, 2000.

Warsh, Lewis. *The Angel Hair Anthology*. Co-edited with Anne Waldman. New York: Granary Books, 2001.

————. *Avenue of Escape*. Brooklyn, N.Y.: Long News Books, 1995.

————. *Information from the Surface of Venus*. New York: United Artists Books, 1987.

————. *Part of My History*. Toronto: Coach House Press, 1972.

————. *The Maharajah's Son*. New York: Angel Hair Books, 1977.

————. *The Origin of the World*. Berkeley, Calif.: Creative Arts Book Company, 2001.

————. *The Suicide Rates*. Eugene, Ore.: Toad Press, 1967.

————. *Touch of the Whip*. Philadelphia, Pa.: Singing Horse Press, 2001.

Welish, Marjorie. *Casting Sequences: Poems*. Athens, Ga.: University of Georgia Press, 1993.

————. *Else, In Substance*. Providence, R.I.: Paradigm Press, 1999.

————. *Handwritten: Poems*. New York: Sun Press, 1979.

————. *The Annotated "Here" and Selected Poems*. Minneapolis, Minn.: Coffee House Press, 2000.

————. *The Windows Flew Open*. Providence, R.I.: Burning Deck Press, 1991.

————. *Word Group*. Minneapolis, Minn.: Coffee House Press, [2004].

Secondary Sources

Allen, Donald, ed. *The New American Poetry*. New York: Grove Press, 1960.

Altieri, Charles. "Ann Lauterbach's 'Still' and Why Stevens Still Matters." *Wallace Stevens Journal* 19.2 (Fall 1995): 219–33.

————. *Self and Sensibility in Contemporary American Poetry*. Cambridge, England: Cambridge University Press, 1984.

Armantrout, Rae. "Feminist Poetics and the Meaning of Clarity." In *Artifice and Indeterminacy: An Anthology of New Poetics,* 287–297. Tuscaloosa, Ala.: University of Alabama Press, 1998.

Baker, Peter. *Obdurate Brilliance: Exteriority & the Modern Long Poem*. Gainesville, Fla.: University Press of Florida, 1991.

Baraka, Amiri. *The Autobiography of LeRoi Jones / Amiri Baraka*. New York: Freundlich Books, 1984.

Bedient, Calvin. "Breath and Blister: The Word-Burns of Michael Palmer and Leslie Scalapino." *Parnassus: Poetry in Review* 24, no. 2 (2000): 170–96.

Bernstein, Charles. *Close Listening.* New York: Oxford University Press, 1998.

Berrigan, Ted. *Selected Poems.* New York: Penguin, 1994.

Bettridge, Joel. Review of Marjorie Welish's *The Annotated "Here" and Selected Poems. Chicago Review*: 130–133.

Bloom, Howard, ed. *John Ashbery: Modern Critical Views.* Chelsea House Publishers: New York, 1985.

Butterick, George, ed. *Charles Olson and Robert Creeley: The Complete Correspondence.* Santa Barbara, Calif.: Black Sparrow Press, 1980.

Campbell, P. Michael, ed. *Palmer / Davidson: Poets and Critics Respond to the Poetry of Michael Palmer and Michael Davidson.* Berkeley, Calif.: Occident Press, 1992.

Carmela Ciuraru, ed. *First Loves: Poets Introduce the Essential Poems That Captivated and Inspired Them.* New York: Scribner, 2000.

Clay, Stephen, and Rodney Phillips. *From a Secret Location on the Lower East Side: Adventures in Writing, 1960–1980.* New York: Granary Books, 1998.

Collins, Martha. "Under the Nest" (review of Ann Lauterbach's *On a Stair*). *Field: Contemporary Poetry* 58 (Spring 1998): 91–101.

Davidson, Michael. *The San Francisco Renaissance: Poetics and Community at Mid-Century.* New York: Cambridge University Press, 1989.

Davis, Jordan. "Interview with Kenneth Koch." *American Poetry Review* 25, no. 6 (Nov-Dec 1996): 45–53.

Diggory, Terence and Stephen Paul Miller, eds. *The Scene of My Selves: New Work on New York School Poets.* Orono, Maine: The National Poetry Foundation, 2001.

Duberman, Martin. *Black Mountain: An Exploration in Community.* New York: W. W. Norton, 1994.

Entwistle, Alice. "Creeley and Crane: 'The Kick / of the foot against.'" *The Cambridge Quarterly* 27.2 (1998): 87–106.

———. "'For W. C. W.,' 'Yet Complexly': Creeley and Williams." *English: The Journal of the English Association* 50.197 (Summer 2001): 127–48.

Faas, Ekbert. *Robert Creeley: A Biography.* Hanover, N.H.: University Press of New England, 2001.

Fink, Thomas A. "The Poetry of David Shapiro and Ann Lauterbach: After Ashbery." *American Poetry Review* 17.1 (1988): 27–32.

Finkelstein, Norman. "The Case of Michael Palmer." *Contemporary Literature* 29 (Winter 1988): 518–537.

Foster, Edward, ed. "Lewis Warsh: Interviews, Essays, New Work." *Talisman: A Journal of Contemporary Poetry and Poetics* 18, (Fall 1998): 33–82.

"France Honors Kenneth Koch with the Insignia of the Order of Arts and Letters." Published online at frenchculture.org (May 12, 2000).

Fraser, Kathleen. *Translating the Unspeakable: Poetry and the Innovative Necessity.* Tuscaloosa, Ala.: The University of Alabama Press, 2000.

Frost, Elisabeth A. "Signifyin(g) on Stein: The Revisionist Poetics of Harryette Mullen and Leslie Scalapino." *Postmodern Culture: An Electronic Journal of Interdisciplinary Criticism* 5, no. 3 (May 1995).

Gilson, Annette. "Disseminating 'Circumference': The Diachronic Presence of Dickinson in John Ashbery's 'Clepsydra.'" *Twentieth Century Literature: A Scholarly & Critical Journal* 44.4 (1998): 484–505.

Golding, Alan. *From Outlaw to Classic: Canons in American Poetry.* Madison, Wis.: University of Wisconsin Press, 1995.

Gooch, Brad. *City Poet: The Life and Times of Frank O'Hara.* New York: Knopf, 1993.

Hinton, Laura, and Cynthia Hogue. *We Who Love to Be Astonished: Experimental Women's Writing and Performance Poetics.* Tuscaloosa, Ala.: University of Alabama Press, 2002.

Howe, Susan. *My Emily Dickinson.* Berkeley, Calif.: North Point Press, 1985.

Jarnot, Lisa, Leonard Schwartz, and Chris Stroffolino, eds. *An Anthology of New (American) Poets.* Jersey City, N.J.: Talisman House, 1998.

Jarnot, Lisa. "On Identity." *Passages* 6, 1998. Published online on wings.buffalo.edu.

Kalleberg, Garrett. "A Form of Duration" (review of Ann Lauterbach's *And for Example*). *Denver Quarterly* 29.4 (1995): 98–109.

Kane, Daniel. *All Poets Welcome: The Lower East Side Poetry Scene in the 1960s.* Berkeley: University of California Press, 2003.

Kaufmann, David. "Repetition, Noise and Pleasure, or Why I Like John Yau and Lisa Jarnot." Published online at chnm.gmu.edu.

Keller, Lynn. "'Just one of / the girls:-- / normal in the extreme': Experimentalists-to-Be Starting Out in the 1960s." *Differences: A Journal of Feminist Cultural Studies* 12.2 (2001): 56–63.

Kevorkian, Martin. "John Ashbery's *Flow Chart*: John Ashbery and the Theorists on John Ashbery against the Critics against John Ashbery" *New Literary History: A Journal of Theory and Interpretation* 25, no. 2 (Spring 1994): 459–76.

Landrey, David. "Robert Creeley's and Joel Oppenheimer's Changing Visions." *Talisman: A Journal of Contemporary Poetry and Poetics* 23–26 (2001-2002): 49–63.

Leddy, Michael. "'See Armantrout for an Alternate View': Narrative and Counternarrative in the Poetry of Rae Armantrout." *Contemporary Literature* 35.4 (1994)": 739–760.

Lehman, David, ed. *Beyond Amazement: New Essays on John Ashbery.* Ithaca: Cornell University Press, 1980.

―――. *The Last Avant-Garde: The Making of the New York School of Poets*. New York: Doubleday, 1998.

Lowell, Robert. "Eye and Tooth." In *Life Studies and For the Union Dead*. New York: The Noonday Press, 1964.

McCabe, Susan. "Stevens, Bishop and Ashbery: A Surrealist Lineage." *The Wallace Stevens Journal* 22.2 (Fall 1998): 149-68.

McHugh, Heather. "Love and Frangibility: An Appreciation of Robert Creeley." *American Poetry Review* 26.3 (May–June 1997): 9–16.

Mullen, Harryette. "Poetry and Identity." *Telling It Slant: Avant-Garde Poetics of the 1990s,* edited by Steven Marks and Mark Wallace, 27–31. Tuscaloosa, Ala.: University of Alabama Press.

Olson, Charles. "Projective Verse." In *Selected Writings*. New York: New Directions, 1966.

Pack, Robert, Donald Hall, and Louis Simpson, eds. *New Poets of England and America*. New York: Meridian Books, 1957.

Padgett, Ron, *Handbook of Poetic Forms*. Teachers & Writers Collaborative, New York, 1987.

Palmer, Michael, ed. *Code of Signals: Recent Writings in Poetics*. Berkeley, Calif.: North Atlantic Books, 1983.

Perelman, Bob, ed. *Writing / Talks*. Carbondale: Southern Illinois University Press, 1985.

Peterson, Jeffrey. "The Siren Song of the Singular: Armantrout, Oppen, and the Ethics of Representation." *Sagetrieb* 12.3 (1993): 89–104.

Quinney, Laura. *The Poetics of Disappointment: Wordsworth to Ashbery*. Charlottesville, Va.: University Press of Virginia, 1999.

Rapaport, Herman. "Signs and Effigies: Michael Palmer's 'Notes for Echo Lake.'" *North Dakota Quarterly* 55.4 (1984): 286–300.

Rifkin, Libbie. "'My Little World Goes on St. Mark's Place': Anne Waldman, Bernadette Mayer and the Gender of an Avant-Garde Institution." *Jacket* 7. Published online at jacket.zip.com.au/jacket07.

——. *Career Moves*. Madison, Wis.: University of Wisconsin Press, 2000.

Ross, Andrew. *The Failure of Modernism: Symptoms of American Poetry*. New York: Columbia University Press, 1986.

Russo, Linda. "Real and Imagined Muses: *The Angel Hair Anthology*." HOW2 1.7 (Spring 2002). Published online at www.bucknell.edu/stadler_center/HOW2.

Schultz, Susan M, ed. *The Tribe of John: Ashbery and Contemporary Poetry*. Tuscaloosa, Ala.: University of Alabama Press, 1995.

Schultz, Susan. "Visions of Silence in Poems of Ann Lauterbach and Charles Bernstein." *Talisman* 13 (1994): 163–77.

Shapiro, David. *John Ashbery, An Introduction to the Poetry*. New York: Columbia University Press, 1979.

Shetley, Vernon. "The New York School of Poetry." *Raritan: A Quarterly Review* 18.4 (Spring 1999): 130–44.

Shoptaw, John. *On the Outside Looking Out: John Ashbery's Poetry*. Cambridge, Mass.: Harvard University Press, 1994.

Smart, Christopher. *Jubilate Agno*. In *The Norton Anthology of Poetry*. Edited by Ferguson/Salter/Stallworthy, 4th ed. New York: W. W. Norton, 1996.

Snyder, Gary. "How to Make Stew in the Pinacate Desert: Recipe for Locke & Drum." In *The Back Country*. New York: New Directions, 1968.

Spahr, Juliana. "'Love Scattered, Not Concentrated Love': Bernadette Mayer's Sonnets." *Differences: A Journal of Feminist Cultural Studies* 12, no. 2 (Summer 2001): 98–120.

Stein, Gertrude. *Lectures in America.* Boston: Beacon Press, 1935.

———. From "What Are Master-pieces and Why Are There So Few of Them." *Context: A Forum for Literary Arts and Culture* 5 (2000): Published online at www.centerforbookculture.org.

Stevens, Wallace. *The Necessary Angel: Essays on Reality and the Imagination.* London: Faber & Faber, 1960.

Tassoni, John Paul. "Play and Co-option in Kenneth Koch's *Ko, or a Season on Earth*: 'Freedom and the Realizable World!'" *Sagetrieb: A Journal Devoted to Poets in the Imagist/Objectivist Tradition* 10, no. 1–2 (Spring–Fall 1991): 123–32.

Tuma, Keith. "An Interview with Michael Palmer." *Contemporary Literature* 30 (Spring 1989): 1–12.

Vickery, Ann. "Finding Grace: Modernity and the Ineffable in the Poetry of Rae Armantrout and Fanny Howe." *Revista Canaria de Estudios Ingleses* 37 (November 1998): 143–63.

Vickery, Ann. *Leaving Lines of Gender: A Feminist Genealogy of Language Writing.* Hanover, N.H.: Wesleyan University Press, 2000.

Ward, Geoff. *Statutes of Liberty.* New York: St. Martin's Press, 1993.

Wasserman, Rosanne. "Marianne Moore and the New York School: O'Hara, Ashbery, Koch." *Sagetrieb: A Journal Devoted to Poets in the Imagist/Objectivist Tradition* 6, no. 3 (Winter 1987): 67–77.

Wolf, Reva. *Andy Warhol, Poetry and Gossip.* Chicago: University of Chicago Press, 1997.

Wright, Amy. "Poetics of Parallel Space: An Interview with Lisa Jarnot." *Sniper Logic* 8 (2000): 54–58.

Yau, John. "Beware the Lady: New Paintings and Works on Paper by Susan Bee." Published online at epc.buffalo.edu/authors (March 27, 2002).